WORLD CLASS

Measuring Its Achievement

WORLD CLASS
Measuring
Its
Achievement

Peter L. Grieco, Jr.

PT Publications, Inc.
4360 North Lake Blvd.
Palm Beach Gardens, FL 33410
(407) 624-0455

Library of Congress Cataloging in Publication Data

Grieco, Peter L., 1942-
        World class; measuring its achievement / Peter L. Greico, Jr.

        ISBN 0-945456-05-0
        1. Cost control. 2. Just-in-time systems. 3. Quality control.
I. Title.
HD47.3.G76   1990
658.5'6--dc20

                                                90-7122
                                                CIP

TABLE OF CONTENTS

FOREWORD

Becoming competitive as a **World Class** company in the global market place begins with the establishment of a base line. This base line is the mark from which a company will measure its progress. In the rush to implement new business and management philosophies, many companies forget this critically important and basic step. This book was written to assist companies in taking that necessary and critical step to becoming a **World Class** company.

Measuring the achievement of **World Class** status is a way of measuring the extent to which a company adheres to the principles of Total Quality Control and advocates employee empowerment. These attributes are the foundation of success. We can no longer ignore them. In order to take first place in world competition, we must develop a management philosophy which gives responsibility and authority to all levels and functions of a company. Such a company should have a vision and a strategic plan to make it come true. This adds up to a Total Business Concept (TBC), a philosophy which advocates driving all waste out of a company. Only when this happens can a company truly call itself **World Class**.

At present, there are a number of prestigious awards given to companies which achieve **World Class** quality status. The oldest such award is the Deming Prize, but rivaling it in importance is the

Malcolm Baldrige National Quality Award, named after the late Secretary of Commerce. Even if you never plan to apply for the award, it is an excellent foundation to use the assessment in this book as a benchmark against the required qualifications.

The book you are about to read is the type of book you need whether you are thinking about Supplier Certification, Set-Up Reduction, Bar Coding, etc. Companies can no longer implement such programs without looking at the whole picture. Completing the assessment in this book provides not only the whole picture, but a detailed picture of each function within the company and the impact that **World Class** business philosophies will have upon them. It is the best way for you to stay competitive, even to survive, in a rapidly changing world.

Jerry W. Claunch
West Palm Beach, FL

ACKNOWLEDGEMENTS

I would like to take this opportunity to thank all the people who have helped in the development of this book, particularly Jerry Claunch, Senior Vice President of Professionals for Technology, Inc. (ProTech), who was instrumental in getting this project off the ground. More capable help came from other members of our consulting staff: Michael W. Gozzo, Chip Long, Phil Stang (for his cartoon), Mel Pilachowski, Wayne Douchkoff and Paul Hine. I would like to note my appreciation here for their contribution in doing research, developing assessment questions, reviewing the work in progress and adding value to the final product.

Most importantly, I would like to thank my very special son, Kevin Grieco, for using his talent to create the artwork and cover design.

Another pillar of support has been provided by Pro-Tech's office staff: Rita Grieco, Leslie Echelson, Dawn Souby, and Theresa Spingola.

Special thanks also to Steven Marks for his continued fine editorial assistance, patience and guidance in establishing a measurement (finally!) for World Class success.

WORLD CLASS

Measuring Its Achievement

CHAPTER ONE

World Class Company Excellence

The aim of this book is to assist companies moving along the path which results in the achievement of **World Class Status**. Every journey, according to an ancient Chinese sage, begins with the first step. And we believe that the first step toward excellence begins with finding out where you are standing at the moment. Many companies that explore the realm of World Class Status start down the path with the latest advice and books. With a burst of enthusiasm, they begin implementing a JIT/TQC program. But, before long, they find themselves in an area which their books and advice have never mentioned. They are lost. One of the members of the company's exploration team takes out a "map" and pores over it for several long minutes.

Finally, another member of the expedition asks the fateful question, "Where are we?"

The map-gazer looks up and points to a mountain on the horizon. "See that mountain over there? As near as I can figure, we're on top of it."

This is what happens to companies which have not established their present position as a benchmark from which they can measure their progress. This is what this book will help you establish. The purpose of the **World Class Assessment** is to help a company gather information about its current status in order to establish a baseline from which improvements can be identified and quantified. In addition, the **World Class Assessment** is also a procedural system for measuring performance and a process for setting objectives which keeps a company's attention focused on priority issues. Those three reasons for conducting a **World Class Assessment** bear repeating:

- **Establishing a baseline.**

- **Instituting a procedural system for measuring performance.**

- **Implementing a process for setting objectives and priorities.**

Each company must develop **World Class** strategic goals in order to prosper and even survive. However, not many companies spend time assessing their business market or capability. Out of the 40,000 companies which requested and received applications for the Baldridge Award for Quality, named after the late Secretary of

Commerce, only 60 completed the application. Can it be that the amount of work required to achieve **World Class Status** exceeded the amount of resources which these companies were willing to use? Not all companies think that the effort is not worth the price. Motorola, Milliken and Xerox, all recent winners of the Baldridge Award, embarked upon aggressive programs where they committed significant resources to improve their **World Class Status**. Florida Light and Power spent a considerable amount of dollars on consulting, education and training over a few years in their effort to win the Deming Award (named after pioneer J. Edwards Deming), which is awarded in Japan to companies excelling in quality.

Achieving **World Class Status** is not a singular event. It is a journey through time for a company, a series of events that add up to a process. As a journey, it is also a search for a new way of working, similar in many respects to the journey that Christopher Columbus made to discover the new world. This new world will be a workplace which allows a company to be competitive, best in its class, profitable and fun to work for. The **World Class** company will anticipate the market; it will not be market driven. It will understand its own business; it will not be involved in business analysis. It will use creative thinking, not strategic planning. It will be a company which uses its organization to capacity. That is the beginning of the achievement of **World Class Status**.

But, what does a **World Class Assessment** have to do with **World Class Status**? And what exactly is **World Class Status** and why does a company need to work toward it? Let's look first at why a company should achieve **World Class Status**.

THE BENEFITS
OF WORLD CLASS EXCELLENCE

The benefits of World Class Excellence are legion and, unlike the benefits of business philosophies of the past, the real power of these benefits comes from how they integrate with and reinforce each other. Furthermore, some of the benefits will be less obvious than others. Therefore, to single out one benefit at a time can be misleading, if its value is not understood in a larger context. In this larger context, a company can expect to reap the benefits below as World Class Excellence is approached:

1) **LOWER TOTAL COST OF PRODUCTS**
   A result of better relations with suppliers, lower inventory costs, lower cost of quality and better coordination between purchasing and customer, design, production and planning.

2) **GREATLY IMPROVED SUPPLIER SERVICE**
   The price of material is only one part of Total Cost and not as important as the delivery of zero-defect material which flows continuously through the plant to the customer.

3) **GREATLY IMPROVED QUALITY**
   Not only because of the emphasis on quality, but because we realize the impact of savings as a result of less inspection and more prevention will result in more profit.

4) **BETTER DESIGN**

New products are not developed behind closed doors and then thrown over walls to unprepared and sometimes obstinate manufacturing departments. Design engineering now works with purchasing, production and shop floor people to make designs that work and that are far less expensive and capable of being produced. Suppliers should also be included very early in the design process.

5) **IMPROVED ADMINISTRATIVE EFFICIENCY**

As paperwork diminishes and people truly communicate and work together, administrative coordination develops naturally and wasteful tasks diminish. When you work closely with suppliers and customers, you will also experience less paperwork.

6) **INCREASED PRODUCTIVITY**

In terms of all personnel in an organization, better flow of material, quicker set-up and shorter lead times, and elimination of wasted time, machines, material and operations. Productivity is not the same as automation. Productivity is not people working harder, but people working more intelligently. Specifically, it is more output with the same input.

To be more specific, a company should at least expect gains in the areas below to fall within these ranges:

Improved Customer Service Performance	**30-50%**
Total Cost of Quality Savings	**60-80%**
Total Inventory Reduction	**25-75%**
Lead time Reductions	**50-75%**
Labor Effectiveness Increases	**10-30%**
Reduction in Set-Up Time	**50-70%**
Reduction in Warehouse Space Requirements ..	**35-50%**
Cost of Sales Reduction	**10-20%**
Supplier On-Time Delivery Improvement	**50-70%**
Improved Inventory Turns	**50-300%**

WHAT JIT/TQC HAS DONE
FOR SOME AMERICAN COMPANIES

A floppy and hard-disk drive manufacturer was able to reduce the amount of work-in-process inventory on the floor from 22 days to one day. This resulted in a 50 percent decrease in stock room space and a savings of $500,000 on purchased parts alone during the first year of the JIT/TQC program. This company was also able to triple its sales from $40 million to $120 million while decreasing the space needed to build and ship the products from 86,000 square feet to 67,000 square feet.

Florida Power and Light Company, in its quest to win the Deming

Prize for Quality, has over 1400 quality circles. Due to this massive commitment to quality, customer complaints have been cut in half, lost-time injuries are down 34 percent and a power plant was completed $600 million under budget in six years or less than half of the industry average.

Using set-up reduction methods, the Friction Materials Division of Bendix reduced the set-up time on a drilling machine from 12 hours to one hour and 10 minutes. Another machine's set-up time went from 65 minutes to 12 minutes. Set-up time reductions in excess of 80 percent were accomplished with cash outlays of as little as $700. As a result of these improvements, the company has significantly increased production capacity and gained the flexibility to meet customer demands.

By employing cellular technology, General Housewares has reduced the lead time on the covers for its commercial cookware from 25 days to six hours, a 99 percent reduction!

SECO Products, a manufacturer of food service and healthcare products, embarked on an aggressive JIT/TQC program with an emphasis on set-up reduction. The company lowered lot sizes from eight weeks to one week; reduced overall inventory by $500,000, or 60 percent, with a bottom line impact of approximately $160,000; and, improved customer on-time delivery performance by 25 percent.

A $160-million auto parts manufacturer implemented a JIT/TQC program along with other cost-cutting programs and witnessed a 32 percent reduction in finished-goods inventory. In addition, they determined that they no longer needed a 460,000-square-foot warehouse.

Harley-Davidson Motor Co., Inc. of Milwaukee have named their JIT/TQC program M.A.N., or Materials-As-Needed. Under M.A.N., Harley has reduced in-process and in-transit inventory at their York, PA, assembly plant by $20 million.

General Motor's Buick City plant in Flint, Mich., reduced inventory on hand and in transit by $23 million, from $48 million to $25 million.

General Electric has begun JIT/TQC programs in roughly 40 different plants. The results: some pilot programs at various facilities report reductions in inventory by up to 70 percent with labor productivity gains of up to 35 percent.

A $4-million producer of plastic products for automotive manufacturers found that it could simplify a procedure on one of its presses and reduce the set-up time by 50 percent. Other small changes amounted to $25,000 in capital expenditures, but netted almost $75,000 in savings.

An auto parts manufacturer also worked diligently to remove wasted actions and procedures. Adopting JIT/TQC concepts, they cut the set-up time on one machine from 7 minutes, 13 seconds to 7 seconds. On another machine, set-up time dropped from 26 minutes to 3 minutes.

A lumber company witnessed a cut in lead-time at one plant from three weeks to three days; a cut of six weeks to two days another plant; and, a remarkable cut of 30 days to minutes at yet another plant because of a new factory floor layout which incorporated JIT/TQC concepts.

An electronics manufacturer has used a JIT/TQC program that

identifies defective parts and shuts down production. Their system has been successful to the tune of building products that are "virtually 100 percent" free of defects.

A food processing plant reduced set-up time from four hours to 10 minutes by using teams consisting of hourly employees and management representatives. This same company improved inventory accuracy from 42 percent to 92 percent in just 15 weeks.

TOTAL BUSINESS CONCEPT (TBC): THE OBJECTIVE OF WORLD CLASS EXCELLENCE

World Class Excellence begins with the implementation of Just-In-Time/Total Quality Control (JIT/TQC) using a parallel internal and external approach. What exactly is JIT/TQC and why is the Total Business Concept necessary for **World Class Excellence**?

JIT/TQC is a frequently discussed, but infrequently applied approach to excellence which seeks to minimize waste, obsolescence and complexity. It is a business concept which includes Marketing, Sales, Finance, Engineering and Administrative support personnel. It is not a vastly complicated program nor a computer software system. Indeed, it is new in the sense of being a revolutionary vision of the workings of a company.

JIT/TQC is in part a resurrection, a redefinition of objectives and an unrelenting commitment to them. It is not, repeat **not**, an inventory reduction program, but includes reduction in a holistic approach to all company operations. **World Class Status** is a quest to solve the causes of wasted time, equipment and labor throughout a company, all of which results in wasted money.

We often liken JIT/TQC's far-reaching implications to a spider's web as noted in **MADE IN AMERICA:** *The Total Business Concept* (ISBN 0-945456-00-X) by Peter L. Grieco, Jr., and Michael W. Gozzo. Touch one silken strand and the entire web vibrates, alerting the spider to a possible meal. Likewise, JIT/TQC alerts plant managers to the presence of problems that we Americans have too often covered with large stocks of inventory and wasteful operations in the belief that foreign competition will be minimal and that our economy will expand at a comfortable rate.

What, then, is a simple definition of **World Class Status?**

**The right item in the right place at the right time
in the right quantity
and meeting customer requirements,
every time and everywhere in the company
at the lowest total cost.**

This could mean the right information as well as the right amount of raw material. Most companies adopting JIT/TQC are more surprised by the indirect effects than the obvious ones. We can't emphasize enough that a total commitment to quality and efficiency at every step by all workers, whether on the shop floor, in administration pools, in warehouses or in managerial offices, will produce effects that nobody had originally surmised.

Thus, **World Class Status** is a mind-set, or a total business philosophy, which can help companies worldwide who find themselves in the throes of the greatest overhaul since the Industrial Revolution. This overhaul has been forced upon us by our own neglect while, at the same time, nations capable of producing higher quality at lower cost swallowed up our market share. Many international corporations, scrambling to find new ways to increase productivity, improve quality and cut costs, have moved their operations off-shore in years past to obtain a low unit cost. Most found out that this strategy did not pan out in the way which was expected.

The principal goal of this book is show you how we can get our operations back on the road to productivity. And that will take an honest appraisal of why we have problems. Indeed, it will mean finding the problems, rather than reacting to the symptoms. Additionally, we wish to make it clear that we are in a *crisis* of quality. And that will demand another honest self-evaluation of why we have grown accustomed to extensive rework, excess inventory sitting on plant floors, poor shipping performance from suppliers and past due orders.

There is no question in our minds that everyone in business, whatever the industry, whatever the operation, can benefit from a **World Class Assessment** which incorporates business strategy objectives. The results will be significant whether the company achieves the highest level or simply improves business from its present benchmark.

CHAPTER TWO

What's Your JIT/TQC IQ?

In the previous chapter, we stated that a company cannot expect to achieve **World Class Status** until it makes an honest appraisal, or self-evaluation, of its present situation in order to establish a benchmark. This chapter introduces the first step in **World Class Assessment** — determining how well a company comprehends the underlying philosophy needed to achieve World Class Status.

The following self-evaluation was developed by M. Scott Myers, Director of the Center for Applied Management and we would like to thank him for allowing us to use his evaluation. He wrote the **JIT/TQC Learning Instrument** to aid individuals and groups in the identification of topics most in need of clarification and to illustrate the various interrelated factors influencing the philosophy of continuous improvement. Mr. Myers based the questions on various sources of information regarding opinions and facts about JIT/TQC management philosophy and techniques. In most cases, more than one choice may be appropriate.

There are no "wrong" answers to this evaluation in the sense that you have failed if you did not identify the "right" answer. Our suggested answers are on Page 253. Consider your company: Knowing where you are headed is every bit as valuable on your path to **World Class Excellence** as is knowing all the right answers. The **JIT/TQC Learning Instrument** will alert you to opportunities, not mistakes.

1   **The goal of a company is to** _____
   a)   Keep inventory low.
   b)   Make money now and in the future.
   c)   Capture a larger share of the market.
   d)   Make high quality products.
   e)   Reduce operating expenses.
   f)   Keep as many people employed as possible.
   g)   Survive.

2   **As I understand it, JIT/TQC applies to** _____
   a)   Product design.
   b)   Supplier development.
   c)   Raw material receiving.
   d)   Production flow.
   e)   Preventive maintenance.
   f)   Space utilization.
   g)   Automation of production.
   h)   Inventory management.

i)   Set-up technology.

j)   Eliminating time clocks.

k)   Use of quality circles.

l)   Bar coding.

m)   Problem recognition.

n)   Problem recording.

o)   Problem solving.

p)   Permissive management.

q)   Reusable containers.

r)   Finished Goods distribution.

s)   Goal-setting.

t)   Defect prevention.

u)   Personal time off.

v)   Operating expense.

w)   Teamwork.

x)   Area management (housekeeping).

3   **The application of JIT/TQC principles can _____**

a)   Lower inventory costs.

b)   Improve manufacturing processes.

c)   Change the company culture.

d)   Make established rules and procedures obsolete.

e)   Reduce waste.

f)   Result in greater administrative flexibility.

g)   Be useful as a problem-solving process.

4   **Which of the following problems might be eliminated or reduced through JIT?**

a)   Capacity constraints (bottlenecks).

b)   Too many models.

c)   Improper parts transfers.

d)   Quality problems.

e)   Engineering changes.

f)   Inventory shrinkage.

g)   Labor problems.

h)   Inaccurate bill of materials.

i)   Inadequate training.

j)   Poor supplier performance.

5   **Compared with JIT/TQC/TPI (Total Product Involvement) processes now finding widespread application, conventional manufacturing management systems are found to be wasteful in their approach to _____**

a)   Quality.

b)   Design.

c)   Purchasing.

d)   Job assignment.

e)   Plant configuration.

f)   Equipment selection.

g)   Maintenance.

h)   Scheduling.

i)   Accounting.

j)   Product-line development.

k)   Material handling.

l)   Material control.

m)   Shop floor control.

n)   Employee motivation.

6   **Which of the following functions should be actively involved in JIT/TQC?**

a)   Personnel.

b)   Manufacturing.

c)   R & D.

d) Sales.
e) Purchasing.
f) Accounting.
g) Data processing.
h) Maintenance.

7 **Legitimate excuses for not using JIT include which of the following?**
a) Uncooperative suppliers.
b) Delay production.
c) Unavailability of software.
d) Lose control of inventory.
e) Low volume operation.
f) Job shop batch operations.
g) Doing OK without it.
h) Opposed by union contract.
i) All of the above.
j) None of the above.

8 **Which of the following staff functions might require fewer people under JIT/TQC?**
a) Maintenance.
b) Production control.
c) Materials management.
d) Quality assurance.
e) Manufacturing engineering.

9 **Which of the following staff functions might require more involvement under JIT/TQC?**
a) Industrial engineering.
b) Purchasing.
c) Accounting.

    d)   Manufacturing engineering.
    e)   Design engineering.

10   **The more informed workers are, the more likely they are to have ideas for** _____
    a)   Controlling defects.
    b)   Improving delivery performance.
    c)   Cutting set-up time.
    d)   Reducing operating expenses.

11   **Operator involvement in set-up reduction is encouraged by** _____
    a)   Teaching them the principles of set-up reduction.
    b)   Teaching them the techniques of motion and time charting and analysis.
    c)   Getting their ideas pertaining to procedures.
    d)   Providing an environment of approval that allows them to apply new procedures.
    e)   Providing day-to-day guidance, coaching and encouragement.
    f)   Giving open recognition to individuals and groups for any and all improvements.
    g)   Rewarding major contributors with a financial bonus or day off with pay.

12   **Moving work stations closer together reduces several kinds of waste and cost including** _____
    a)   Transit time.
    b)   Queue time.
    c)   Transit inventory.
    d)   Queuing inventory.

e) Space.

f) Defect detection.

g) Problem-solving barriers.

h) Communication and teamwork barriers.

13 Smaller lots and inventories can lead to _____

a) Reduction of waste and rework.

b) Quality improvements.

c) Enhanced worker involvement.

d) Better process yield and productivity.

e) Worker anxieties about job security.

f) Increased awareness of causes of errors and delays.

g) Reduced operating expense.

14 Production lead time usually consists of which of the following?

a) Engineering design.   [   ]

b) Production time. (Run) [   ]

c) Set-up time.   [   ]

d) Queue time.   [   ]

e) Move time.   [   ]

f) Wait time.   [   ]

Place an "M" in the bracket following the element of lead time that usually consumes the most time, and place an "L" after the element that usually takes the least time.

15 A thoughtfully planned factory should preserve and enhance flexibility through a combination of _____

a) Early introduction of Flexible Manufacturing System.

b)   Simple, low-cost dedicated machines.
c)   Costly equipment capable of easy moving and rapid set-up.
d)   Adaptable human effort.
e)   Decertification of labor unions.

16   Classify inventory as "sitting" or "moving":

		Sitting	Moving
a)	Raw materials inventory	[ ]	[ ]
b)	Finished goods inventory	[ ]	[ ]
c)	Stockroom inventory	[ ]	[ ]
d)	Handling material	[ ]	[ ]
e)	Run time	[ ]	[ ]
f)	Queue time	[ ]	[ ]
g)	Inspection delays	[ ]	[ ]
h)	Safety stock	[ ]	[ ]
i)	Transit time	[ ]	[ ]
j)	Set-up time	[ ]	[ ]
k)	Backflush time	[ ]	[ ]
l)	Machine repair time	[ ]	[ ]

17   As lead times and buffer stocks are reduced, operations must move toward _____

a)   Shorter production runs.
b)   Fast changeovers.
c)   Tight process control.
d)   Total preventive maintenance.
e)   Frequent small deliveries.
f)   Synchronized scheduling.
g)   Smaller, more flexible equipment.
h)   Multiple copies of bottleneck equipment.
i)   Arranging equipment into compact flow lines.

18 **Small inventory is desired because of its direct or indirect impact on** _____

a) Carrying costs—interest, storage, handling, etc.
b) Identification of defects.
c) Facilitating engineering changes.
d) Due date performance.
e) Investment per unit.
f) Margins.
g) Forecast validity.
h) Cash flow.
i) Return on investment.
j) Net profit.

19 **Successful supplier development includes** _____

a) Receiving deliveries on time.
b) Assuring high quality in purchasing material.
c) Having redundant suppliers.
d) Overcoming traditional adversary relationships.
e) Providing supplier training where necessary.

20 **Kanban, a Japanese word meaning "easy-to-read card," is used to** _____

a) Signal the forward flow of material.
b) Make a quick count of inventory.
c) Prevent a pile-up of WIP.
d) Signal a call for help.
e) Facilitate defect detection.
f) Help maintain an orderly workplace.

21   Small job shops, which already resemble cellular manufacturing, usually gain little by rearranging equipment, but can improve flexibility by _____

a)   Reducing set-up times.

b)   Becoming more rigorous in machine maintenance.

c)   Splitting and overlapping lots.

d)   Improving defect detection techniques.

e)   Chopping lead times through customer development.

f)   Sharpening competitive analysis capability.

g)   Acquiring larger, more versatile equipment.

22   Classify each of the constraining conditions _____

		Leader-ship	Logis-tical	Behav-ioral	Environ-mental
a)	Limitations in material, time, space and equipment	[ ]	[ ]	[ ]	[ ]
b)	Careless or counter-productive behavior	[ ]	[ ]	[ ]	[ ]
c)	Outside factors such as government, weather and economy	[ ]	[ ]	[ ]	[ ]
d)	Managerial attitudes, assumptions, policies, business strategies	[ ]	[ ]	[ ]	[ ]

23   The terms "backflushing" in manufacturing parlance means _____

a)   Returning to the original manufacturing process.

b)   Counting the inventory.

c)   Subjecting the WIP to an acid wash.

d) Salvaging the unused work in process.

e) Deducting the material represented in a complete unit from the BOM of the unit.

24 "Burn-in" refers to an electronics manufacturing process for _____

a) Testing a product under stress conditions.

b) Causing a product to fail (or not fail) through simulated aging or stress conditions.

c) Stamping performance specs onto a product during manufacturing.

d) Accelerating the production rate to maximum capacity.

e) Crystallizing a final production procedure.

25 Cycle time refers to _____

a) Amount of time material spends in house.

b) Time between units in repetitive manufacturing.

c) Amount of time an operator devotes to an operation.

d) Worker time plus idle time per operation.

e) The life cycle of a product.

f) Time between recurring events, applied to anything.

26 Invisible inventory refers to _____

a) Paperwork and all kinds of wasteful bureaucracy.

b) Reprocessed waste.

c) Inventory lost through shrinkage.

d) Material in warehouse storage.

e) Inventory in route from supplier.

27   **Area management (housekeeping) includes** _____
a)   Removal of everything from work area not immediately needed.
b)   Removal of excess inventory and tools not in use.
c)   Removal of trash and excess personal effects.
d)   Removal of backup machines.
e)   Keeping the floor and equipment free of dirt and dust.
f)   Creating a special place for personal belongings.
g)   Assigning specific work areas to individuals.
h)   Painting a line around each person's area.
i)   Following work rules.
j)   Restricting workers to their areas.
k)   Support shops such as tool rooms, die shops and maintenance shops.
l)   Maintaining production data.

28   **Area management serves the following purposes** _____
a)   Improve quality.
b)   Shorten set-up times.
c)   Streamline material flow.
d)   Enhance morale.
e)   Please customers.
f)   Encourage participation and problem-solving.
g)   Promote safety.
h)   Keep track of tools.
i)   Improve visibility of conditions.

29 **The status of shop floor operations and materials can be seen at a glance by visual controls such as** ____

a) Workplace organization.
b) Signal lights.
c) Dials and gauges.
d) Kanban systems.
e) Number of standard containers.
f) Halted conveyors.
g) Idle work stations.
h) Operator deployment.

30 **Lights can be used to signal** ____
a) Machine malfunctions.
b) Parts out of spec.
c) Out of parts.
d) Tool change needed.
e) Normal set-up required.
f) Normal maintenance.
g) Supervisor required.
h) Coffee or lunch break.
i) Relief operator needed.
j) Anticipated problem.

31 **Methods for finding and eliminating problems include** ____
a) Ouija boards.
b) Pareto analysis.
c) Fishbone charts (CEDAC).
d) Identifying defect patterns in workpiece.
e) Identifying time patterns of defect occurrence.
f) Identifying malfunctioning tools or equipment.
g) Asking for advice from others.

32   **Japanese manufacturers have achieved their competitive advantage through _____**

    a)   Fostering a sense of partnership with customers, suppliers and employees.

    b)   Extensive use of robots.

    c)   Widespread use of quality circles.

    d)   Attempting to promote lifetime employment.

    e)   Placing more emphasis on people than on capital equipment.

    f)   Modernization of plants with post-war American aid.

    g)   Operating equipment at higher rates of speed.

    h)   Sharing company success with employees.

    i)   Designing and fabricating production equipment in-house.

    j)   Uniform compensation systems tied to company profits.

    k)   Placing quality above all other criteria of excellence in manufacturing.

    l)   Keep the equipment running 24 hours a day.

    m)   Emphasizing long-term over short-term goals.

    n)   Sophisticated inventory control systems.

    o)   Maintaining large economy batches of inventory.

    p)   Modern structures with highly sophisticated equipment.

    q)   Maintaining clean, orderly work places.

    r)   Minimizing inventory at all stages of procurement and production processes.

    s)   Integrating quality considerations into every phase of engineering and production.

33 **One reason Japanese workers typically oversee the operation of more machines than their U.S. counterparts is _____**

a) The cost of Japanese labor is greater compared to the lower cost of their capital equipment.

b) The operation of many machines enriches workers' jobs by giving them a greater sense of responsibility.

c) They make more extensive use of equipment monitoring systems and simple materials handling equipment.

d) Workers feel it is their patriotic duty to out-perform foreign competitors.

e) There is a greater shortage of skilled operators in Japan.

34 **Workers in progressive Japanese plants are usually responsible for _____**

a) Keeping their workplace clean.

b) Keeping their machines in working order.

c) Maintaining output and quality.

d) Helping fellow workers.

e) Resolving grievances and employee conflicts.

f) Correcting minor problems.

g) Monitoring and adjusting equipment.

h) Looking for ways to minimize disruptions.

i) Conducting preventive maintenance.

j) Looking for ways to improve efficiency.

35   **Japanese managers "think quality into" their products by** ____

    a)   Designing the product with quality criteria as guidelines.

    b)   Developing machine specifications, methods and standards with quality in mind.

    c)   Involving their manufacturing and industrial engineers in quality planning

    d)   Training production workers to maintain quality standards.

    e)   Having production workers make quality checks on parts before assembly.

    f)   Encouraging production workers and quality inspectors to correct any quality problems that may arise.

    g)   Encouraging feedback from and to production workers, quality inspectors, salespeople, vendors and customers.

    h)   Having field organizations in many cases reporting to the manufacturing manager (rather than to sales manager).

    i)   Screening incoming parts and materials and giving feedback to suppliers.

    j)   Working with suppliers to determine the causes of problems and helping them to solve them.

    k)   Instructing employees of supplier companies.

    l)   Developing suppliers to deliver zero defect materials.

36   **The "root of all evil," according to Japanese manufacturing managers, is** ____

    a)   Man's inherent greed and selfishness.

b)   Protective tariffs imposed by foreign importers.

c)   The escalating cost of labor.

d)   An insufficient inventory.

e)   An excessive inventory.

f)   A dirty and disorderly workplace.

g)   Underutilized employee talent.

h)   Machine breakdowns.

i)   Lack of promotional opportunities.

37   SMED is an acronym for _____

a)   Simulated Manufacturing with Electronic Data.

b)   Set-up Maximization Empirically Derived.

c)   Single Minute Exchange of Die.

d)   Simplified Manufacturing thru Employee Decisions.

38   Set-ups apply to which of the following operations?

a)   Processing.

b)   Inspection.

c)   Transporting.

d)   Storage.

e)   Cocktails.

39   External die change (EDC) refers to set-up work _____

a)   Engineered outside the organization.

b)   Prepared while operation is in process.

c)   That can be performed only when operation is stopped.

d)   Engineered by outside consultants.

e)   Prepared outside normal working hours.

40   Internal die change (IDC) refers to set-up work _____

a)   That can be performed only when operation is stopped.
b)   Engineered within the organization.
c)   Performed by machine operator.
d)   Conducted while operation is in process.
e)   Conducted during regular working hours.

41   In your company, how would you rank set-up costs?   (1 = highest)

a)   [   ] Resources used in manufacture of dies.
b)   [   ] Time and effort required by set-up.
c)   [   ] Space required to store dies.
d)   [   ] Rehearsal of set-ups.
e)   [   ] Maintenance of dies.
f)   [   ] Lot sizes.

42   Which of the following SMED concepts are advanced by Shigeo Shingo?

a)   The most important step in implementing SMED is distinguishing between internal and external set-ups.
b)   Normal set-up times can usually be reduced 30-50 percent by separating internal and external procedures.
c)   By adopting new perspectives, operations performed on internal set-ups can often be converted to external set-ups.
d)   Once internal and external set-ups are clearly distinguished, each can usually be shortened by further streamlining.

e) Set-up changes should allow defect-free products to be produced from the very start.

f) The ideal set-up change is no set-up at all.

g) It is important to cut set-up times and diminish lot sizes while simultaneously maintaining even flow.

h) The SMED system is the most effective method for achieving Just-In-Time production.

i) Set-up is one key to moving toward future technologies— robotics and advanced automation.

j) Machines can be idle, workers must not be.

k) If you can't figure out how to do something, talk it over with your machines.

43 **The economic-lot concept lost its justification with the development of _____**
a) SPC.
b) MRP/MRP II.
c) SMED.
d) FMS.
e) SQC.

44 **Work simplification espouses which of the following principles?**
a) Every job is capable of being improved.
b) Jobs that are functioning well should be improved.
c) When a job is functioning well, don't try to change it.
d) The ultimate improvement is to eliminate the task altogether.
e) Work Simplification works best when it's tied to a paid suggestion system.

45   **The five-step pattern in Work Simplification includes which of the following (number 1 thru 5 in consecutive order):**
  a)   [   ]   Locate your quality problems.
  b)   [   ]   Select a job to improve.
  c)   [   ]   Locate branches of excess inventory.
  d)   [   ]   Get all the facts.
  e)   [   ]   Develop the preferred method.
  f)   [   ]   Challenge every detail.
  g)   [   ]   Establish problem-solving teams.
  h)   [   ]   Install it and check results.

46   **Match the appropriate flow-process symbol with each of the five operations listed below:**

  a)   Store   _____
  b)   Transport _____
  c)   Delay   _____
  d)   Inspect   _____
  e)   Change   _____

47   **People working next to each other in a linear or U-shaped production line serves to _____**
  a)   Minimize materials handling.
  b)   Facilitate supervisory control.
  c)   Provide better feedback on quality.

d) Keep the freeloaders in line.
e) Enhance communications.
f) Produce ideas for improvement.
g) Improve ability to shift tasks between workers.

48 What is the impact of each of the following operations?

		Add Value	Add Cost
a)	Counting it.	[ ]	[ ]
b)	Moving it.	[ ]	[ ]
c)	Improving it.	[ ]	[ ]
d)	Expediting it.	[ ]	[ ]
e)	Eliminating it.	[ ]	[ ]
f)	Searching for it.	[ ]	[ ]
g)	Storing it.	[ ]	[ ]
h)	Simplifying it.	[ ]	[ ]
i)	Inspecting it.	[ ]	[ ]

49 MRP (Materials Requirements Planning) is a computer system with the following elements ____

a) A production schedule (what to make).
b) Bill of material (the parts required).
c) A shop schedule (production flow in the plant).
d) A capacity plan (How much capacity required).
e) Reliability index (estimated rejects).
f) On-hand inventory (what you have now).
g) New requirements (what you have to go out and get).

50   **JIT and automation strategies are compatible, particularly if automation is in the form of simple and "homemade" devices to** _____
    a)   Measure.
    b)   Hold.
    c)   Identify.
    d)   Locate.
    e)   Index.
    f)   Receive.
    g)   Align.
    h)   Orient.
    i)   Pull forward.
    j)   Protect.
    k)   Adjust.
    l)   Record.

BONUS QUESTIONS

51   **Under JIT/TQC conditions, computer tracking of inventory becomes less necessary because** _____
    a)   The product doesn't spend enough time in the plant for multiple inventory transactions.
    b)   Kanban batches approximate current inventory.
    c)   Lack of rework minimizes abnormal flow paths and times.
    d)   Counting of small batches of inventory is more efficiently done by operators.
    e)   The flow of product is so short and disciplined that inventory is invisible.

52   Before investing in new equipment, _____

a)   Consider alternative manufacturing methods.

b)   Redesign product to off-load bottleneck.

c)   Improve set-up methods.

d)   Improve yield.

e)   Improve tools or gages.

f)   Train operators.

g)   Reduce employees' wages.

h)   Consider make vs. buy.

i)   Incorporate special quality demands.

j)   Improve preventive maintenance.

53   If visiting a plant, which of the following would you consider relevant to manufacturing excellence?

a)   Flexible layout for Raw Material to Finished Goods flow.

b)   Evidence of cross-training.

c)   Balanced mix of people by gender, age, race, etc.

d)   Evidence of operator initiative and influence.

e)   Visibility of problems and conditions.

f)   Evidence of quality improvement efforts.

g)   Preventive maintenance.

h)   Producible product designs.

i)   Small lots or flexibility in process.

j)   Process capability.

k)   Clean and orderly work areas.

l)   Schedule balance or stability—bottlenecks, etc.

m)   Spirit or level of motivation.

n)   Fluid communication processes.

o)   System simplicity.

54   **Which of the following strategies might be useful for introducing JIT principles into an organization?**

a) Appoint a project leader to champion JIT implementation.

b) Form a coordinating team with representatives from every department.

c) Set up a common learning experience for everyone.

d) Attending professional seminars outside or within the organization.

e) Joint reading and discussion of publications on JIT.

f) Field trips to factories with JIT.

g) Creating models or simulations of JIT production lines that all can observe.

h) Videotaped demonstrations of JIT for group learning experience.

i) Establish a pilot project before converting the whole factory.

j) Have consultants install JIT and explain it to the work force.

k) Piggy-back on existing quality circles or other team efforts.

HOW DID YOU DO?

The list of preferred answers appears before the index in the back of the book. If we had assigned a point value of two points for each preferred answer, scoring would have looked like the example on the next page.

Number of Correct Answers

90-100   **Excellent knowledge of JIT/TQC and why it is important to achieving World Class Status.**

75-89   **Adequate knowledge of JIT/TQC, but in need of more training and education in order to achieve World Class Status.**

below 74   **Less than adequate knowledge of JIT/TQC. Definite need for extensive training and education in order to become competitive.**

Our objective with this assessment is to help a company evaluate the knowledge of its people in order to provide it with a starting point. It is not important whether you score 100 or 50. What is important is that there is a need to improve continuously if you wish to remain competitive in the world marketplace. Mr. Myers' questions bring to light the confusion which exists today around the understanding of business and customer requirements. I'm sure we could have a healthy discussion over whether or not a particular answer is correct or not. If we did, however, we would be missing the objective. You need to review your responses not only in the light of remaining competitive, but as an indicator of the presence or absence of a vision for continuous improvement.

I would recommend sending this evaluation to people at all levels of your company. Take the responses and do a correlation in order to determine the company's level of expertise. From this information, it is possible to figure out how much and what kind of training and education is needed to enhance the JIT/TQC position of your company. This will be a company-wide effort. Changing a company's culture to incorporate a **World Class** mentality is not accomplished by a few people.

Having completed the self-evaluation of your JIT/TQC knowledge, the next step is to conduct an assessment of your company in all business areas. The next chapter addresses the issue of how to conduct a **World Class Assessment**.

CHAPTER THREE

How to Use the World Class Assessment

We perform surveys, audits and assessments of a company to determine its present status, where it has been and where it needs to be. Traditional methods of assessing a company's performance, however, no longer provide an accurate indication of an organization's viability and survivability. It stands to reason that the new philosophy of conducting business, the Just-In-Time/ Total Quality Control (JIT/TQC) philosophy, requires a new way of reviewing each company since it must now grow from within.

The **World Class Assessment** has been designed to reflect new process methods, practices and customer/supplier relations. The assessment is based on the relationship which exists when all departments, functions and personnel provide the building blocks. The **World Class Assessment** will aid your company in determining the capabilities and opportunities of each of its functions. In particular, this assessment will alert your company to:

1. How much waste is present in company operations and related activities. Waste, today, is too often accepted as a given and absorbed into overhead costs. This is a reactive way of thinking and must change as we compete in the world market.

2. How actual performance compares to the stated goals and objectives. Observing this variance is instrumental in making new plans which will enable a company to take corrective action immediately.

WHO SHOULD CONDUCT THE WORLD CLASS ASSESSMENT?

This assessment will serve to move us away from the strategic plan to creative thinking by the whole company. During the last ten to fifteen years, companies have limited their competitive advantage by only concentrating their efforts on sustaining market shares, as Michael Porter has documented in his writings. Preoccupation with competitiveness squeezes innovation out of the picture. The **World Class** company must be innovative to survive. This creativity provides the basis for improvement.

We suggest a steering group be formed to conduct the **World Class Assessment**. This group should have its "finger on the pulse" of the real business issues. The burden should not rest solely on one department. Each department should work closely with all the other departments in an assessment of company operations which is based on total cost and a company-wide perspective. There is a strong need for different functional groups to build bridges between each other and to work together in the implementation of the findings of this assessment. The first step is to conduct the assessment in the following chapters.

Departments which should participate in the assessment are Finance, Purchasing, Manufacturing, Engineering, Design, Sales, Marketing, Direct Labor and possibly Suppliers. The **World Class Assessment** is a team effort to evaluate the internal and external aspects of a company. It is vital for the assessment team to be made up of individuals from a number of disciplines within a company. This is done so there will be input from a number of areas which will reflect the interconnected nature of the Total Business Concept. It is advisable to seek outside professional help to facilitate the assessment team since objectivity is crucial to the assessment's success and many people are protective of their own area this early in the process.

WHEN SHOULD THE WORLD CLASS ASSESSMENT BE CONDUCTED?

The answer to when the **World Class Assessment** should be conducted is very simple. **Immediately!** It is never too early to start. By using the process outlined in the next chapter, it should only take eight to ten days per site to complete the assessment. If you think that is a long time, then think about how much longer time will seem when the competition has overtaken your position in the world marketplace.

HOW TO COMPLETE THE PROCESS

You will be required to gather a great deal of information about the current status of your company. Some sections of the World Class Assessment require a simple "yes" or "no." Other questions ask for definitions or descriptions of present and future plans. Still other questions require financial information and performance estimates. In the case of performance measurements, you may have difficulty accurately quantifying a particular measurement. Make the best estimate possible. It is far better to have an approximation than no answer at all. We recommend that actual data be used whenever possible.

It is advisable for a company to use a team approach while conducting the **World Class Assessment**. It will be as a team that you eventually evaluate the gathered information and begin to take the action necessary to correct deficiencies. Of equal importance is the necessity of *not* having personnel assess their own department. You can only guess at the results.

There are inherent problems with teams. Whenever a lot of cooks are stirring the broth, there will be arguments over what ingredients are best. How do you form and manage an assessment team in which you reap the benefits of a diverse group while not stifling individual creativity? How can Purchasing sit down with Marketing, Engineering, Production and Quality and assess their operations?

The answer is to establish ground rules, goals, objectives and a sense of direction early in the process. You must infuse a sense of vision, responsibility, authority and accountability in the group which gathers to work on a task. We must move toward a company environment in which previously separate areas are able to merge and transform their roles. The **World Class Assessment** will be a process of fusion, rather than fission. Energy is created as different departments work closer and closer together, as the barriers between them slowly break down, just as our sun creates energy by fusing hydrogen atoms into ones of helium. In the process of fusion, your company will move from ignorance and confusion about **World Class Excellence** to the adoption of a **World Class Mind-Set**.

Remember also, that the assessment should be completed in an established number of days. Avoid allowing an assessment team to study or plan the project to death. We call these people "StrateJITs" — People who study the big picture to death and who normally come up with results which are Bull JIT. Usually, this is the result of people becoming so involved with the process that they can't see the forest for the trees.

Once tasks and people are identified with time tables established, you are ready to conduct the assessment. It is imperative that start and finish dates should not be canceled and that there should be 100% participation. Nothing stops the momentum of interaction more quickly than one or two people not being involved. Members immediately start to question the company's commitment to the process and begin to feel that the commitment is not at hand.

Let me share a story about a company which conducted the **World Class Assessment**. The company began the process by holding a briefing session attended by over fifty key employees. At the session, management stated that the company must start the process in order to meet the competition. Two weeks later, management decides that the cost of educating people and using consulting services to reach the required skill levels is too high. The plan was shelved. What message does that give to the people who work at the company? It's "OK" to talk about improvement, but it's not "OK" to show your commitment with dollars. When you decide to proceed with the assessment, be *sure* you are prepared to go forward with the process.

" I've decided to talk about improvement, just don't discuss time or dollar commitments! "

One last rule about the assessment teams and their administration. The best teams are those in which a high level of motivation exists within the team members. This approach, which can be aided by the services of outside consultants, creates a greater sense of ownership, acceptance and commitment within the team. The process most often fails because teams have not been trained in solving problems, but in treating symptoms. Equally important is to create an environment in which everybody can speak without fear of reprisal. It is true that there are basic rules for a team process. Nevertheless, there are differences in culture, attitude and company history which have effects on the program. Our **World Class Assessment** has been developed to be flexible enough to cover all types of industries, processes and business applications.

CHAPTER FOUR

The
World Class
Assessment

The **World Class Assessment** is contained in the next nine chapters. Each of the chapters focuses on one or more areas of inquiries. For this reason, it is strongly recommended that you conduct the assessment in the order which is presented. Latter chapters build upon information gathered in earlier chapters.

To aid you in the assessment's completion, we have preceded each topic by one or more paragraphs which explain the importance of the questions which follow. These comments will also help direct your information gathering activities. Further comments have been inserted where we have deemed it appropriate to explain unfamiliar concepts.

COMPANY PROFILE

Company Name   _____

Address _____

_____   Zip_____

Telephone_____   FAX _____

Company Is A Division Of   _____

MANAGEMENT

Name	Title	Function
_____	_____	_____
_____	_____	_____
_____	_____	_____
_____	_____	_____
_____	_____	_____

GENERAL COMPANY BACKGROUND

This section provides a snapshot of what products the company or plant manufactures and the volume produced and sold each year. The snapshot also includes a picture of the company's organizational structure, or who works where and how these people are organized. Often, an organizational chart and a breakdown of employees by department will provide information about a company's profile.

Management in firms typically have a minimum of seven to eight levels (and even more) between the top and bottom rungs. **World Class** firms, on the other hand, normally operate with a maximum of three levels of management. Consequently, when you want to make a decision in a **World Class** environment, you can do so much more quickly. Of course, that will necessitate a shift in companies from decision-making by the few at the top to decision-making by those who are most clearly affected by the need for a change or an improvement. That shift in attitude may result in a paring down of the number of levels of management as an ultimate goal.

The 1990s are going to require extensive changes. Management will need an agenda like the one below:

THE 1990S AGENDA
FOR THE WORLD CLASS COMPANY

LEADERSHIP and COMPANY CULTURE

FROM	TO
Centralized direction	Decentralized management
Autonomous functional areas	Integrated company
Rigid plans	Plans which adapt to changes

MANAGEMENT EFFECTIVENESS

FROM	TO
Do it faster	Do it smarter
Planning and scheduling on national scale	Planning and schedulng on local scale

HUMAN PRODUCTIVITY

FROM	TO
Duplication of functions	Integration of functions
Spend to meet the budget	Budget to meet total cost

CUSTOMER/SUPPLIER RELATIONSHIPS

FROM	TO
Adversaries	Strategic partners based on trust and commitment
Top-down initiative	All-level initiative

MIND-SET and ATTITUDES

FROM	TO
Individual	Teamwork
Specialist	Generalist

1. General Business Classification

   ____ Manufacturing ____ Repetitive ____ Process
   ____ Other

   SIC Code_____

2. Major Product(s):_____

   _____

   _____

3. Company Ownership: ____ Private ____ Public

   Susidiary_____ Independent_____

   If susidiary, parent company?

   _____

   Traded on _____Exchange

4. Total Sales this year $_____

   Next year projected $_____

   % Domestic_____ % Foreign_____

   Fiscal year ends on what date_____

5. Number of Years in Business_____

6. Organization Chart (Please attach copy)

7. Dun and Bradstreet rating_____
   (if available)

8.   Number of Employees:

_____ General Management

_____ Finance and Accounting

_____ Sales and Marketing

_____ Engineering (Design and Manufacturing)

_____ Production and Inventory Control

_____ Factory Direct

   _____ 1st Shift   _____ 2nd Shift   _____ 3rd Shift

_____ Quality

_____ Purchasing

_____ Traffic

_____ Factory Supervision

_____ Human Resources

_____ Materials

_____ Total this site

_____ Union

_____ Non-union

Strikes in last 5 years?   _____ Yes _____ No

Employee turnover ratio _____%

PRODUCTION CONSIDERATIONS

Completing this section will help you identify production lines, equipment or processes which are most suitable for the implementation of CIP (Continuous Improvement Process) programs, especially Set-Up Reduction, Design for Producibility (DFP) and Supplier Certification. Some companies, for example, conduct their Set-Up Reduction programs by part or process; other companies break down their program by machine. The latter is especially true in discrete environments where a particular machine changes frequently to produce different items. A company may also want to apply their Set-Up Reduction program to a family of items. Perhaps there is an item group or a "bread and butter" family of products which generates the most customer orders or dollars affecting the plant. If so, start there with this phase of the **World Class** process.

DFP is a new technology which is garnering a tremendous amount of interest today. Although little has been written so far about the tooling and process changes required, we are sure that there will be many seminars, articles and books which will shed some light on this opportunity. Ultimately, DFP will tie into "time to market" and thus allow companies to compete far more successfully in the world market. We think that "the future is in applying DFP rules — *today!* "

A successful Supplier Certification program demands that the internal flow of material be as orderly as the flow from internal/external suppliers. What is true for the supplier side is also true for the customer side. You will be required to view each part of your company as a certified supplier capable of on-time delivery of 100 percent quality products in the quantity needed by other internal departments as well as external customers. We also believe that it would be an excellent idea to get your suppliers to conduct a **World Class Assessment** as well.

1. Production Facilities Include:

   Single site_____   Multiple Site_____

Plant	Organized Labor Yes No	Location	Product(s) Manufactured	Production Activity %Fabri. %Assem.	Plant (Sq Ft)
_____	__ __	_____	_____	_____ _____	_____
_____	__ __	_____	_____	_____ _____	_____
_____	__ __	_____	_____	_____ _____	_____
_____	__ __	_____	_____	_____ _____	_____

2. Typical Equipment/Process Used in Plant(s)

Plant Name	Equipment	Process
A. _____	_____	_____
B. _____	_____	_____
C. _____	_____	_____
D. _____	_____	_____

3. Unique or Special Equipment/Process Used in Plant(s)

   A. _____

   B. _____

   C. _____

   D. _____

4. "Standard" versus "Special" Production

    "Special" (custom) Production is _____% of Total

5. Number of Product Lines Manufactured_____

6. Patented Items _____% of total sales

PERFORMANCE MEASUREMENTS

The problem with today's traditional performance measurements is that they are usually inaccurate because they often fail to compare actual data against predicted performance. Accuracy is best obtained through a system of measurement which has real-time information about both internal and external operations. Current information coupled with a documented past is the most useful information in plotting trends of the future.

The principal thrust of this section of the **World Class Assessment** is to emphasize a total cost-oriented approach, rather than a price-oriented approach for financial measurements. Unfortunately, most companies today don't have the tools in place to calculate total cost completely. Therefore, as you can probably guess, they don't calculate any portion of the total cost. This approach continually erodes away the basis for improvement. We must use a model for total cost early in the process, no matter how rough it may be. It is better to be approximately right than precisely wrong.

We must also not look at price alone, but quality, quantity and delivery, in seeking to optimize profits. We should measure variances against cost, not price when evaluating our profitability.

These two principles work in tandem with the basic principles of a **World Class Company**, that is, build to demand and eliminate excess inventory and wasteful operations. The direction of the future is to incur costs only when material or operations add value to the product we are building.

As we continue to streamline our plant through the reduction of costs, we will find that financial controls actually become easier to manage and report. In the **World Class Company**, inventory could be accounted for simply by looking at the level of work-in-process. By changing traditional manufacturing and accounting practices, we may be able to have more control than before and provide for a major shift in the process to change a company's culture.

Determine the value or status of the performance measurements that are available through on-going reporting. If a measure is not available, please estimate.

FINANCIAL INFORMATION	(DATE) CURRENT	(DATE) 6 MOS	(DATE) 12 MOS	FORMULA USED
Sales Revenues (annualized $)	_____	_____	_____	_____
Cost of Sales (annualized $)	_____	_____	_____	_____
Average Inventory $	_____	_____	_____	_____
Inv. Carrying Cost	_____	_____	_____	_____
Purchasing Costs (annualized $)	_____	_____	_____	_____

FINANCIAL INFORMATION	(DATE) CURRENT	(DATE) 6 MOS	(DATE) 12 MOS	FORMULA USED
Direct Labor Costs (annualized $)	_____	_____	_____	_____
Indirect Labor Costs (annualized $)	_____	_____	_____	_____
Factory Overhead Cost	_____	_____	_____	_____
Corporate Burden (annualized $)	_____	_____	_____	_____
Cost of Quality	_____	_____	_____	_____
Scrap $/%	_____	_____	_____	_____
Rework $/%	_____	_____	_____	_____
Overtime Premium Costs (annualized $)	_____	_____	_____	_____

Performance Measure	Actual	Goal	Estimated	On-Going Reporting	Formula Used
Business Plan Performance	_____	_____	_____	_____	_____
Sales Plan Performance	_____	_____	_____	_____	_____

Inventory Turnover Ratio

The measurement of inventory turns is perhaps one of the best methods for determining the progress toward **World Class As-**

sessment. Most companies today are struggling to achieve three or four inventory turns a year. That is four months of inventory on hand. We expect that companies will have to raise their Inventory Turnover Ratio to 14 turns, 26 turns, 36 turns or more per year in order to be competitive in the future.

Performance Measure	Actual	Goal	Estimated	On-Going Reporting	Formula Used
Inv. Turns/Yr	_____	_____	_____	_____	_____

Customer Delivery Performance

In a **World Class Company**, the issue at hand is to manufacture only what you sell. To do otherwise means that you are increasing inventory items. We advocate that you establish a goal of a 100% to customer requirement service level. Once established, you measure actual shipping versus the shipping plan daily, weekly, monthly, quarterly and year-to-date. Remember to include past due orders which should be rolled forward into the current month. Your company's performance should be measured on the sum of past due orders and the current month which will require you to make up the backlog as well as the current month's orders.

Performance Measure	Actual	Goal	Estimated	On-Going Reporting	Formula Used
Customer Delivery Performance	_____	_____	_____	_____	_____

Forecasting Accuracy

Planning for production and supplier schedules depends on accurate, short-term forecasting. The closer forecasts are to actual demand, the closer a company is to attaining a "pull" system of manufacturing, a principal component of **World Class Status**.

At Macintosh, Steve Jobs refused to provide us with a forecast. He would simply say, "If you know all forecasts are wrong, why do you want one?" In reality, the most accurate forecasts are those with a short horizon — the day you sell a product, the next day or the same day you ship it.

Performance Measure	Actual	Goal	Estimated	On-Going Reporting	Formula Used
Forecasting Accuracy	_____	_____	_____	_____	_____
Forecasting Error Within Mfg. Lot	_____	_____	_____	_____	_____
Master Schedule Adherence	_____	_____	_____	_____	_____
Prod. Load Past Due	_____	_____	_____	_____	_____

Supplier Delivery Performance

On-time delivery compares the actual receipt date to the confirmed delivery date. Remember that early delivery is just as costly as late delivery. If you're receiving parts two or three days ahead of schedule, inventory will rise and you will have to pay the costs of carrying it. The higher the percentage of suppliers delivering on-time and the smaller your delivery window, the closer you come to **World Class Status**. This is a measurement which can be calculated for delivery as a whole and for each individual supplier or buyer. Improvement is gained as more and more suppliers come over to Just-In-Time delivery. The goal is for each supplier to deliver on the day committed.

Performance Measure	Actual	Goal	Estimated	On-Going Reporting	Formula Used
Supplier Delivery Performance	_____	_____	_____	_____	_____

Return on Asset Utilization

This financial measurement is viewed differently in the **World Class** environment. The reasoning that idle time is expensive and that a major asset such as a machine has to pay for itself by producing parts is faulty. The fallacy in this reasoning is that it is based on absorbing labor and overhead for product which is not needed. The logic is "Catch 22" in nature. The more unnecessary the product you make, the more inventory carrying cost you must absorb. All this does is stockpile sub-assemblies or finished goods. Warehousing costs money; the cost of carrying inventory costs money. The two costs probably far exceed the cost of idle machines. The goal is to have each machine ready for production, not necessarily running, 100% of the time. The goal is not to keep people busy, but to have machines available for use.

Performance Measure	Actual	Goal	Estimated	On-Going Reporting	Formula Used
Return On Asset Utilization	_____	_____	_____	_____	_____

Performance Measure	Actual	Goal	Estimated	On-Going Reporting	Formula Used
Shortage List	_____	_____	_____	_____	_____
Labor Utilization	_____	_____	_____	_____	_____
Equipment Utilization	_____	_____	_____	_____	_____

Cost of Quality

Continuous improvement of quality not only moves you toward zero-defect products, but increases savings as well. The cost of quality divides into three classifications — Failure Costs, Appraisal Costs and Prevention Costs. The first two classifications, failure and appraisal, are typical of costs incurred by manufacturers using traditional quality methods. They are the costs associated with products which do not conform to requirements. Prevention costs, on the other hand, are more in keeping with **World Class Excellence**. Not surprisingly, spending more on prevention and less on failure and appraisal costs will increase savings.

The cost of quality is usually greatly underestimated by most companies. When a company has a low level of quality understanding, reported actual costs increase dramatically. As the company approaches **World Class Status,** the reported cost of quality is significantly lower than the average of 32-35% typical of today. When we get lower than this level, we begin to have control over the process. This lower level is also where we want suppliers to be.

Performance Measure	Actual	Goal	Estimated	On-Going Reporting	Formula Used
Cost Of Quality	_____	_____	_____	_____	_____
Failure Cost	_____	_____	_____	_____	_____
Appraisal Cost	_____	_____	_____	_____	_____
Preventive Cost	_____	_____	_____	_____	_____

Record Accuracy

Record accuracy is what we call an "up-front" consideration. There are two reasons for this. One, we exist in an environment where change is the only certainty. It is imperative that the information which we use in planning is up-to-date, as close to a real-time environment as is possible. Two, we can't use up-to-date information that is inaccurate. Amazingly enough, we have heard companies say that every other part that they count in inventory is right on the money. That's only 50 percent; hardly the percentage needed to operate in a **World Class** environment where pinpoint timing and accurate quantity counts are absolutely necessary. You simply can't forecast, plan, schedule or produce without the most basic of all raw materials—accurate information.

Under the MRP II banner of the past, many experts said that **Class "A" Status** was achieved with 95% record accuracy. I wonder how they can run their companies at this level of accuracy. Doesn't this sound like a 2% AQL (Acceptable Quality Level)? A

5% rate of error is totally unacceptable. The only goal for **World Class Status** is 100%. *There is no compromise!*

Performance Measure	Actual	Goal	Estimated	On-Going Reporting	Formula Used
Raw Material	_____	_____	_____	_____	_____
W.I.P.	_____	_____	_____	_____	_____
Finished Goods	_____	_____	_____	_____	_____
Distribution Center	_____	_____	_____	_____	_____

(above measurement based on quantity and physical location)

Routing Accuracy	_____	_____	_____	_____	_____
Bill of Material Accuracy	_____	_____	_____	_____	_____

Traffic and Freight

This measurement will make you look more closely at what it costs you to receive material and to ship your product. Transportation costs are a significant factor. The point, obviously, is to control your costs and find the most economical method of transportation which will lower the total cost of the product. With **World Class Status**, you will be looking for frequent, small lots of material to be delivered when required. This can result in an increase in freight costs, if the carriers are not part of the team.

Performance Measure	Actual	Goal	Estimated	On-Going Reporting	Formula Used

Freight - Inbound (% of Purchase Material):

Performance Measure	Actual	Goal	Estimated	On-Going Reporting	Formula Used
Premium	_____	_____	_____	_____	_____
Air	_____	_____	_____	_____	_____
Rail	_____	_____	_____	_____	_____
Truck	_____	_____	_____	_____	_____
Sea	_____	_____	_____	_____	_____
Demurrage	_____	_____	_____	_____	_____

Performance Measure	Actual	Goal	Estimated	On-Going Reporting	Formula Used

Freight - Outbound (% of sales):

Performance Measure	Actual	Goal	Estimated	On-Going Reporting	Formula Used
Premium	_____	_____	_____	_____	_____
Air	_____	_____	_____	_____	_____
Rail	_____	_____	_____	_____	_____
Truck	_____	_____	_____	_____	_____
Sea	_____	_____	_____	_____	_____
Demurrage	_____	_____	_____	_____	_____

If percent not available, obtain Dollars and calculate.

JUST-IN-TIME/TOTAL QUALITY CONTROL

We believe that, in order to attain **World Class Status**, we must analyze why we have problems—and why our competitors don't. Being as good as our competitors is not enough. Being the best is our objective. We must recognize that we are in a crisis of quality: we've grown accustomed to extensive rework of parts, excess inventory sitting on the plant floor, poor shipping performance from our suppliers and poor customer service.

What companies must do is become committed to quality and productivity at every step. We need a new mind-set about what we're trying to achieve and how we're going to do it.

What is JIT/TQC? It's an approach which seeks to minimize waste, obsolescence and complexity while maximizing customer service at the same time. It is a redefinition of our objectives and an unrelenting commitment to improve. Companies applying, for example, for The Baldridge Award are showing a commitment to achieving **World Class Status**. Winning the award is **World Class**.

World Class Excellence demands that a company achieve the lowest total cost and highest quality possible in order to satisfy customers. You can be sure, that if you are building a good product, somebody else in the world is going to build the same product and compete with you. Do we need to be reminded again about what happened to the camera, television and steel business? Higher volume, more production, better quality—in short, the benefits of JIT/TQC— allow you to grab a larger share of the market today and develop new markets for the future.

The CEO who is dedicated to **World Class** will support the creativity and innovations of his or her people. This individual will tear down the barriers that stifle creative thinkers. People who operate "outside the box" will be rewarded.

Perhaps the best way to determine how close a company is to **World Class Status** is to measure how well it communicates. One of the biggest problems today is the tendency to break companies into small, unilateral cubicles. Members of the same function in a company tend to cluster together under the umbrella of some stand-alone activity. When people cluster, it is not the result of working as a team applying JIT/TQC concepts. It is the result of people attempting to do their jobs within the confines of their own little area which is counterproductive to **World Class** objectives.

The environment of most companies today is reactive. They operate in this manner because that is the way it has always been done. Are they considering, right up front, what is required to produce a new product? Are they considering time to market? If a product is designed and released before its time, companies will spend valuable time and resources in redesigning. Market share will be lost and customer service ignored. A **World Class Manu-facturer** cannot operate in that type of environment. And what is more, external competition is going to beat you to the market. There must be communication among the various functions in order solve a majority of the problems.

American companies have to stop thinking of the firm as a conglomeration of independent departments. Reduced lead-times, reduced lot sizes, group technology, **World Class Excellence**—all of the benefits of JIT/TQC will never be obtained without teamwork and people supporting each other. Lastly, let's not forget our motivation to be **World Class**. Companies have a fight on their hands and JIT/TQC helps them to become stronger and more competitive. The savings we can garner will not only improve our cash flow and make us stronger financially, but will help us to reduce the amount of price increases for our products while still increasing profits. JIT/TQC enables companies to make **top-quality products at the lowest total cost.**

This section is geared toward a review of the level of JIT/TQC in each of your companies today. It can also be used to point out areas which must be addressed in the months and years to follow.

1. What is the company's vision? _____

   _____

   _____

   _____

   _____

2. Does a JIT/TQC charter exist?   Yes____ No____

   If yes: Have performance measurements been formally established to monitor results of the program?

             Yes _____   No _____

   If no, prepare a charter for company buy-in.

3. Is there a JIT Steering Committee? If yes, please check functions involved:

   a. General Manager ____   f. Purchasing   ____
   b. Manufacturing   ____   g. Materials   ____
   c. Engineering   ____   h. Finance/Acct. ____
   d. Quality   ____   i. Marketing/Sales ____
   e. Human Resources____   j. Corporate   ____
   k. Other   ____

4. Have JIT Teams been established? Yes ____   No ____

   If yes: How many ____ How organized: Size _____

   % salaried members ____   % hourly members ____

5. Has any formal training been conducted in _____ ? Check if yes and put in by whom.

   ____ JIT (Just-In-Time) _____

   ____ TQC (Total Quality Control) _____

   ____ Statistical Process Control_____

   ____ Supplier Certification_____

   ____ MRP/MRP II_____

   ____ JIT Purchasing_____

   ____ CIM (Computer Integrated Manufacturing) _____

   ____ Preventive Maintenance_____ _____

   ____ Set-up Reduction _____

   ____ Total Cost_____

_____ Performance Measurements _____

_____ Cost of Quality _____

_____ Team Building _____

_____ Problem Solving _____

_____ Capability Studies _____

_____ Design for Producibility _____

_____ Other_____

6. Is there a reward system for employee involvement teams?

    Yes _____ No _____

    If yes, describe, define plans for future

    _____

    _____

7. Is there a plan to implement Computer Integrated
    Manufacturing (CIM) or components for the company?

    Yes _____   No _____

    If yes, describe:

    _____

    _____

8. Is there cost reporting for make vs. buy/subcontract decision making?

   Yes _____   No _____

9. Is there a committee to make the decision?

   Yes ___ No ___

   Does a formula exist? Yes ___ No ___

   If yes, what is the committee makeup?

   _____

   _____

   _____

   % salaried involvement _____

   % of hourly involvement _____

10. Is there a formal business plan? Yes _____ No _____

11. Is there a formal sales plan?   Yes _____   No _____

12. Is there an aggregate production plan? Yes ___ No ___

13. Does a Management Steering Committee exist for guiding and prioritizing technology acquisition and integration activities? Yes _____ No ___

    What functions are involved? (List them.)

14. Presently, are the efforts directed to areas of highest opportunity? (Highest cost of non-conformance or market growth potential)

    Yes _____ No _____

15. Have areas of greatest potential for improvement been identified with cost/performance baselines.

    Yes _____ No _____

16. Anticipated benefits on major projects and a risk analysis is conducted for all projects.

    Yes _____ No _____

17. Are tracking and reporting performance measures in place for specific improvement projects against original projections with widely visible graphic displays?

    Yes _____ No _____

18. Has the company established islands of technology ?

    Yes _____ No _____

19. Is group technology being employed? Yes ___ No ___

20. Is the application of CAD/CAM being considered or in existence?

    Yes _____ No _____

21. Is Corporate communication established?

    ___ Newsletter
    ___ Regular information meetings frequency _____
    ___ Other means to communicate. Please state: _____

22. Is there a formal Value Analysis Program? Yes ___ No ___

    If yes, describe

    _____

    _____

    Functions involved:

    _____

    _____

    _____

    _____

    % salaried employees _____   % hourly employees _____

23. Is there a formal system of problem solving? Yes ___ No ___

    If yes, describe

    _____

    _____

    Utilized by whom:

    _____

    _____

    _____

INVENTORY CONSIDERATIONS

How important is inventory control? Out-of-control inventories have been likened to a "noose around U.S. industry's neck." Up to 50 percent of a manufacturer's assets are tied up in inventory. This non-productive capital is one of the strongest drains on the vitality of American manufacturing. It is imperative that we begin exploring alternative methods of inventory control, such as those coming under the umbrella of **World Class**. The underlying reasons for inventory reduction are to:

1. Improve your competitive position both domestically and internationally.

2. Eliminate waste (Inventory, Carrying Costs, Physical Space, Material Handling, etc.).

3. Expose unproductive manufacturing processes.

4. Minimize obsolescence.

5. Introduce flexible manufacturing.

6. Respond more quickly to change.

7. Meet customer demands quickly.

Safety stocks only solve one problem at the expense of covering up far more serious problems. Eliminating high levels of inventory will expose hidden problems. Actually dealing with the real problems and not hiding behind walls of inventory allows us to be more flexible/productive in our factories.

This assures us that we will not be trapped with inventories that have become obsolete because our competitors have built a better product. What good is a warehouse of 'prop' planes when everybody wants jets? It's much easier to get rid of a handful of unwanted products than a few hundred or a few thousand or even a few hundred thousands.

One way to speed the evolution toward **World Class** is to have a program which addresses inventory. Then we can mark the progress we are making against a baseline measurement and a goal of opportunity. However, we do not advocate starting to reduce inventory without a program of set-up reduction and lot size reduction. Inventory is directly correlated to the elimination of set-ups and large lot sizes.

1. Inventory levels:

   a. Average total inventory $_____

   b. Total inventory includes the following categories and related levels:

	Dollars	Accuracy
1. Raw Material	_____	_____
2. Maintenance, Repair and operating supplies	_____	_____
3. Work-In-Process	_____	_____
4. Finished Goods	_____	_____
5. Distribution	_____	_____
6. Slow moving	_____	_____
7. Obsolete	_____	_____
8. Other	_____	_____
Total Inventory	_____	_____

2. Is slow moving or obsolete inventory identified by the following?

    A.) On-hand balance exceeds requirements_____

    B.) No requirements_____

    C.) Engineering change order control _____

    D.) Lapsed time since last transaction_____

3. Origin of Inventories (Parts and Assemblies percent/dollars)

    Components Parts/Assemblies

	Components	Assemblies
Total inventory in Purchased Material	_____	_____
Purchased Material for Stock	_____	_____
Purchased Material for Special	_____	_____
Customer Order/Hold	_____	_____
Total inventory in Manufactured Parts	_____	_____
Manufactured for Stock	_____	_____
Manufactured for Special	_____	_____
Customer Order	_____	_____

4. How many Sku's?_____
   Raw Material_____
   Components_____
   Assemblies_____
   Finished goods_____
   Number of pallets?_____
   Raw Material_____
   Components_____
   Assemblies_____
   Finished goods_____

5. What are the present inventory turns based on 12 months cost of sales forecasted divided by on hand inventory?

    <2___ 3-5 ___ 6-9 ___ 10-12 ___ 12-16 ___ 17 ___>____

6.   What are the last two year's inventory turns?

_____ 2 yrs. ago   _____ last year

7.   Dollar value of obsolete inventory?_____

How defined _____

8.   Dollar value of excess inventory? _____

How defined _____

9.   Does trailer or outside storage exist? Yes____ No____

If yes, what is dollar value? _____

10. Is it included in total inventory? Yes____ No____

11. Is there any inventory stored at other locations?
     Yes___ No___

Dollar value at:

$ _____Supplier consigned stock at
               your/their location
$ _____Supplier
$ _____Customers (consignment)
$ _____Distributors
$ _____Other (Make and Hold)

12. Is this included in total inventory? Yes ____ No ____

13. Is there any Zero Valued Inventory? Yes ____ No ____

14. Does Purchasing hold up shipments to meet inventory objectives?
               Yes ____ No ____

15. Who is responsible for total inventory dollars?

   Name_____ Title_____

16. Does a cycle count program exist? Yes _____ No _____

   A.) Hit or miss _____ Tolerance level_____

   B.) Are results used to measure stockroom performance?
   Yes _____ No _____

   C.) Are tolerance levels allowed outside accepted ranges?
   Yes _____ No _____

17. Who is responsible for inventory accuracy?

   Name_____Title_____
   Function_____

18. Who is responsible for physical movement of inventory?

   Name_____ Title_____

19. Is data integrity adequate to reflect all transaction types
   properly?
   Yes___ No____

20. Is an ABC classification provided to assist in establishing
   control procedures and priorities?   Yes___ No____

21. What systematic method exists to correct inventory transaction
   errors?

   _____

   _____

22. What is the history and magnitude of inventory adjustments for
   the last two years? _____   _____

23. Does the company adjust financial results based on inventory adjustments?
Yes___ No____

24. How much downtime does the operation incur as a result of periodic physical inventories? _____ hours
_____ dollars

25. Are the results of physical inventories to book value correct?
Yes___ No____

CHAPTER FIVE

Management Information and Systems

As part of the nervous system of the business, Management Information is a vital part of a company's need to attain **World Class Status**. Many companies, unfortunately, have difficulty accurately describing what types of hardware and software applications they use and who are the personnel who use the tools provided by a system. Over the years, it has been said that the JIT process has made the use of systems obsolete. Nothing could be further from the truth.

The establishment of a long-term systems plan for **World Class** operations needs to recognize each system's aspects and that each aspect is interdependent upon the preceding system. Planning is required to develop **World Class** systems so that information and the building blocks of some systems are maintained. The foundation of **World Class** systems is the capability to capture and process quantities of day-to-day data and paperwork, such as invoices, purchase orders, stock movements, shipping documents, etc. These systems must record the data, provide timely information on customer status — on-hand, on order, delivery — and, perhaps more importantly, update systems which are the input to higher level planning and control.

World Class planning systems must provide data to all functional areas which serve as a basis for short and near term decision making. Material requirements planning is a system which provides specific information regarding what, how many and when certain items are to be made available for sale or higher level assembly in a daily/hourly mode.

Well designed information systems are instrumental in reporting data on time, gaining control of the factory, improving quality, lowering costs and increasing on-time delivery. A sound system design starts with an accurate assessment of requirements made by a team consisting of representatives from, at a minimum, the departments of Data Processing, Finance, Materials Management, Manufacturing, Marketing and Sales. Their task will be to evaluate your present system and find ways to improve it, or replace it, so that you can build a "closed-loop" system which will support **World Class** activities. Such a system is an evolutionary step toward the Factory of the Future and toward Computer Integrated Manufacturing (CIM). These will be the *necessities* of a **World Class Company** in the nineties and beyond.

HARDWARE

1. CPU:

   Manufactured
   by_____Model_____

   Memory Size:_____

2. Disk Capacity_____

3. Tape Drives: (Module/Quantity)_____

4. Printers: (Model/Quantity) _____

5. Terminals: (Model/Quantity)_____

6. Local Area Network _____

7. Personal Computers_____

8. Documentation_____

9. Policy and Procedures _____

SOFTWARE

1. Operating System _____

2. Database Management System_____

3. Communications Software _____

4. Local Area Network_____

5. Financial_____

6. MRP/MRP II_____

7. Forecasting_____

8. CAD/CAM_____

9. Repetitive_____

10. Distribution_____

11. Graphics_____

12. Word Processing_____

13. Electronic Mail_____

14. EDI_____

15. Revision Number_____

16. Documentation_____

17. Other_____

PERSONNEL

1. Programmers (Number/Experience)_____

2. Systems Analysts (Number/Experience)_____

3. Computer Operators (Number/Experience)_____

4. How many "users" operate the computer_____

APPLICATIONS

1. Number of Data Transactions Daily_____

2. EDI Applications_____

3. Real-time or Batch Process_____

4. System Response Time_____

CURRENT SYSTEMS

This part of the **World Class Assessment** requires a company to take stock of the systems being used and how they are utilized. If a new system is being implemented, this section will help you review progress. It is not enough in a highly competitive world merely to purchase and own systems software which never gets used or never gets used properly. When fully implemented and utilized, the systems will provide a company with a window into its operations. The systems will aid companies by showing them how and where to:

- Reduce inventories while maintaining service to the production line.

- Utilize the sales force to increase equipment use while improving customer satisfaction.

- Increase plant capacity in order to maximize profits.

- Lower scrap and rework levels by integrating production control methods.

- Obtain the lowest total cost and how to acquaint Purchasing and Finance with Total Cost Management.

- Show Sales which customers merely provide volume and which provide profits.

This portion of the **Assessment** requires a company to state its future plans for implementing and completing various system applications. We would like to emphasize here that it is important to develop a plan to accomplish the identified task. Far too many implementations remind us of a high-school student writing a 20-page term paper the night before it is due. That is no way to achieve **World Class Status.**

STATUS/EVALUATION

APPLICATION	Manual or Computerized	Software Package	Percent Accomplished	Accuracy of Data	Goal
Inventory Control	_____	_____	_____	_____	____
Bill of Material	_____	_____	_____	_____	____
Materials Requirements Planning	_____	_____	_____	_____	____
Process Routings	_____	_____	_____	_____	____
Shop Floor Control	_____	_____	_____	_____	____
Capacity Planning	_____	_____	_____	_____	____
Purchasing	_____	_____	_____	_____	____
Product Costing	_____	_____	_____	_____	____

Order Entry   _____   _____   _____   _____   ____

Accounts
Receivable   _____   _____   _____   _____   ____

Accounts
Payable   _____   _____   _____   _____   ____

Payroll   _____   _____   _____   _____   ____

General Ledger   _____   _____   _____   _____   ____

Quality   _____   _____   _____   _____   ____

Preventive
Maintenance   _____   _____   _____   _____   ____

C.A.D.   _____   _____   _____   _____   ____

C.A.M.   _____   _____   _____   _____   ____

Distribution
Requirement
Planning   _____   _____   _____   _____   ____

Forecasting   _____   _____   _____   _____   ____

Other (Specify)   _____   _____   _____   _____   ____

   _____   _____   _____   _____   ____

   _____   _____   _____   _____   ____

MATERIALS REQUIREMENT PLANNING

In the execution of **World Class** Materials Requirement Planning (MRP), a company's computer system begins with a 100% accurate bill of material (BOM). As you explode the BOM and move down through the levels, it should be an objective to reduce the number of levels within the BOM structure.

The power of MRP rests in the computer's ability to manipulate massive amounts of data in a *quick and accurate* manner. This manipulation of data determines what material will be pulled at various stages in the manufacturing process and when it should be purchased. Most MRP systems today allow for the allocation of inventory which exists in the store room. In short, MRP allows manufacturers to control a process which is subject to frequent changes in orders, inventory records and bills of material, if the regenerations are performed on a frequent basis. Many of the experts contend that MRP is not needed in the JIT environment. This is definitely not true. MRP serves as the foundation and planning tool; JIT is the execution vehicle. Together, they provide data in a timely fashion for users. This allows companies to determine order quantities using lot size and lead time information. This is a critical area for manufacturers who wish to attain **World Class Status** and is inextricably linked to customer demand.

LEAD TIME, LOT SIZES AND SET-UP REDUCTION FOR WORLD CLASS

The intent of set-up reduction is to reduce production set-up times in order to support a movement toward smaller lot sizes, less lead time and improved productivity. The following principles must be at work in the interaction of these three areas at a **World Class Company:**

1. Smaller lot sizes necessitate faster changeovers of equipment.

2. Smaller lot sizes require more set-ups which places an emphasis on JIT delivery to the operation.

3.   Sound procurement decisions must be based on real need and quality rather than price.

4.   Long set-ups require long runs which translates into higher inventory and associated carrying costs.

5.   Reduced set-ups result in shorter runs which translates into less inventory.

World Class Companies must be able to wean themselves from long production runs in favor of flexible manufacturing. In flexible manufacturing, machine operators must be able to reduce set-up time so that production can quickly change from producing one item to another to dovetail with customer requirements.

LEAD TIME OBJECTIVES

Lead time represents a costly utilization of a wide variety of company resources. Its reduction is both a vital cost of quality and cost reduction opportunity. The following are the objectives of a lead time reduction process at a **World Class Company**:

REDUCE OR ELIMINATE SET-UP.

Set-up is a non-productive, income-using element of lead time. It impedes the response by a company to customer requirements and negatively impacts line and machine efficiency. Furthermore, it increases "buffer" inventory requirements. On a positive note, set-up reduction allows you to unleash all those hidden benefits of producing at lower cost and shorter time.

IMPROVE MATERIAL HANDLING.

Material handling is a non-productive use of resources. It should be minimized using the same principles as employed in set-up reduction. The goal is reduce the quantity of material moved and thus simplify material handling.

MATCH LOT SIZES
TO CUSTOMER DEMAND.

Reductions in lead time allow you to approach the smallest lot size of one part. In essence, the goal is to produce on time exactly what the customer orders. No more, no less!

TIME TO MARKET.

Time to market and throughput reductions accelerate production flow which results in lower inventory carrying costs, lower cost of quality and more manufacturing floor space.

1. Are the company's management goals and objectives clearly stated and understood throughout the organization?
    ____Yes ____No

2. Are key objectives such as inventory performance and customer service levels identified?   ____Yes ____No

3. Are criteria for measurement and adherence established for the following?

    Carrying Costs _____

    _____

    Order Processing Costs _____

    _____

    Backorder Costs _____

    _____

    Labor Rates _____

    _____

    Burden Rates _____

    _____

4. Is there adequate definition, review and approval of the following?

    Demand Forecast _____

    _____

    Master Schedules _____

    _____

Production Plans _____

_____

Reorder Points _____

_____

Safety Stocks _____

_____

5. Master Scheduling:

a. Present method of master scheduling evaluation:

Inventory Level _____

Capacity _____

Labor _____

b. Which of the following are considered in the
       development of master schedule?

____Sales Forecast ____Backlog ____Service/Spare Parts

____Inventory Adjustments ____Capacity Constraints

____Labor Stability

Other_____

c. Which functional area is responsible for master schedule?
_____

d. Master schedule time period used is?
___Weekly ___Monthly

Other_____

e. Master schedule is updated: ____Weekly ____Monthly

Other_____

f. What is master schedule planning horizon?
_____

g. Does an approved demand forecast support the master schedule? ____Yes ____No

h. Does the planning system provide insight to review key component availability prior to releasing a master schedule? ____Yes ____No

6. Requirements Generation:

a. Present method of determining component requirements:

____Regenitive ____Net Change

b. Frequency:_____

c. What lot sizing methods are utilized?

____Discrete ____Period Order Quantity

____Lot for lot ____E.O.Q. ____Wagner Algorithm

____Fixed Order Quantity ____Min/Max

Other_____

d. What material is considered in the availability calculation?

____On Hand ____Floor Stock ____Safety Stock

____Inspection ____Scheduled Receipts

____In Transit Other_____

e. Is anticipated scrap considered?
_____(Loss at Assembly)

How_____

f. Is anticipated shrinkage considered?
_____ (Loss at Receipt)

How_____

g. MRP Reporting:

What reporting presently exists?_____

_____

_____

7. What functions and resources are involved in the preparation of the Master Schedule?

_____ _____

_____ _____

_____ _____

8. Does the master schedule verify work centers for availability prior to planning item requirements? ____Yes ____No

9. Can the system evaluate the total cost of a given production plan so that alternatives can be evaluated?
    ____Yes   ____No

10. Is the planning horizon consistent with item and supplier lead times? ____Yes   ____No

11. Are future resource requirements identified by a long-range production forecast?   ____Yes   ____No

12. Are requirements identified for all stock items?
    ____Yes   ____No

13. Are policies identified to provide purchasing information to change order due dates when item requirements change?
    ____Yes   ____No

PLANS

What are your priorities for implementing new application software?

PRIORITY	APPLICATION	IMPLEMENTATION DATE
1	_____	_____
2	_____	_____
3	_____	_____
4	_____	_____
5	_____	_____
6	_____	_____
7	_____	_____

Describe the key issues as stated by the people that stand in the way to closing the loop:

_____

_____

_____

_____

How to Tell When a Company has World Class Systems

- Utilizes all modules of the system.

- People use the system as an integrated approach.

- Achievement of accuracy is 100% in major categories.

How to Tell When a Company Wants to Have World Class Systems

- Some modules in place.

- Scheduling performed regularly.

- Business not run with data.

- Works issues, doesn't solve problems.

- Blames system for their own problems.

- Heart is in right place and good effort, but results are poor.

How to Tell When a Company Doesn't Have the Foggiest Idea of World Class Systems

• Consistent use of hot lists.

• Lacks a master schedule.

• Lack of closed loop approach.

• No visible measurements in place.

CHAPTER SIX

Application
Detail

BILLS OF MATERIAL

Bills of material accurately list the items used in producing a finished good and the level at which each item is added to the assembly. You can compare a bill to a recipe which lists the ingredients and their proportions. I still wonder why it is a common practice for companies to produce finished goods from inaccurate bills. Some companies use no bills of material at all. The latter case may work for the "cook" who throws a plastic pouch in boiling water, but not for the "chef" who must prepare more elaborate creations.

Just as Julia Childs must prepare an accurate list of ingredients needed to make a complicated meal, so must a **World Class Manufacturer** insist on a 100% accurate bills of material. Incorrect bills lead to faulty planning and execution of the production plan. For example, if a bill lists a component not used in producing a product, either inventory will grow or someone must intervene and cancel an order for that component. If that person forgets or goes on vacation, unnecessary inventory will be procured and stored. Conversely, if a bill does not list a required component, either the finished product will be incorrect or a "catch-up shortage" environment will be created. In either example, it is far easier to maintain an accurate bill of material which negates the need for special handling. The achievement of **World Class Status** will only be possible if your bills are 100% correct.

1. General

    a. Does each item on the bill of material have a unique item number? ____Yes ____No

    Assigned: In-House____   Supplier____   Other____

    If no, how are unique parts identified from one another?

    _____

    _____

    _____

    b. Are items maintained in inventory differentiated by same item number as identified on the bill of material?
    Yes __ No __

    Explain, if no_____

    _____

    _____

c. Are bills of material maintained on computer files?

____Yes   ____No

1. If no, how maintained:_____

_____

2. If BOM is computerized, what are the outputs?

_____

_____

d. Are there written procedures for development and maintenance of the BOM?

    ____Yes   ____No

    If yes, how is compliance audited? _____

    _____

e. Which function maintains BOM's?_____

f. Who uses BOM's?_____

_____

g. How many different BOM files, including hard copies, are kept?

_____

h. Is the BOM used for development of product costs?

    ____Yes   ____No

i. Which techniques apply:

____Modular BOM   ____Option/Substitution/Accessories

____Pseudos   ____Engineering BOM

____Planning BOM   ____Family BOM

____Phantom   ____Other_____

j. Commonality of parts usage is:

____High   ____Moderate   ____Low

k. Is BOM structured to raw material level?

____Yes   ____No

If no, explain how raw requirements are identified:

_____

How many levels?____#

l. Is the BOM used to identify other items such as tooling, fixtures, etc.?

____Yes   ____No

If yes, identify: _____

m. How is product variation documented?_____

_____

n. Are component designators identified in BOM (R.M., F.G., W.I.P., etc.)?   ____Yes ____No

If yes, how are they identified?_____

o. Are bills of material structured according to how product is manufactured?

____Yes ____No

2. File Size and Activity:

a. Total number of end items _____
b. Total number of item master records _____
c. Total number of product structure records (BOM) _____
d. Maximum number of levels in a product structure _____
e. Total number of parts per typical end item _____
f. Average number of new BOM's issued each month _____
g. Average number of BOM changes issued each month ___

3. Engineering Considerations:

a. Is part status identified?____Pre-released ___Released

____Obsolete ____Service Only Other_____

b. Are assembly parts maintained? On Drawing___ Detached___

c. Is there a formal engineering change procedure?

____Yes ____No

If no, explain how engineering changes are documented and controlled:_____

_____

_____

d. Do engineering change orders utilize revision level control?

____Yes ____No

    e. Is an engineering change coordinator utilized?

    ____Yes   ____No

Position reports to:_____

    f. Is there an engineering change review board? __Yes__No

Chairman:_____

Meeting schedule:_____

Closed Loop:_____

    g. Are BOMs reviewed regularly for opportunities to flatten (i.e., reduce) the number of levels?

      ____Yes   ____No

4.   Time period to process engineering change request:

      Hours___ Days___ Weeks___ Months___ Years___

5.   Time period to process engineering change:

      Hours___ Days___ Weeks___ Months___ Years___

6.   Are BOMs audited regularly for accuracy?

      ____Yes   ____No

If yes, how accurate are they? _____

MATERIAL HANDLING

World Class Status is attainable only when material flowing through the plant is carefully planned and controlled. As work progresses from work center to work center, **World Class Manu-facturers** must have the ability to pull, not push product from operation to operation. Since production is based on demand, the master scheduler requires less time to monitor the progress of the material.

Backlogs, productivity variances, machine downtime, scrap and rejects all contribute to today's problems. In order to achieve **World Class Status**, we must insure that the identified problems are eliminated.

First line supervision, thus, has less responsibility to execute the shop schedule since responsibility is given to the floor. Since plans generated by MRP can only be fulfilled if materials are available on time, supervisors must play an active role in the use of Kanban, pull manufacturing, supplier relations, planning, etc. The role of first line supervisors changes to one of the leaders on the shop floor with authority and responsibility.

The object of this section is to material movement and lead time and to drive the process to lot-for-lot production with the support of all functions. A typical method for achieving this would be a pilot project based on product.

1. Present method of inventory record keeping:

    ____Computerized   ____Kardex   ____Manual

    Other_____

2. Is a limited access stockroom concept employed?_____

3. Is part kitting or staging done?_____

    If yes, explain use:_____

    _____

4. Are multiple storage locations per item allowed?_____

5. Are stock locations identified?_____

6. What is the format for stocking location ID?_____

_____

7. What inventory balances are maintained?

_____On-Hand _____In Inspection _____On Hold

_____In Transit   Other_____

8. Manufacturing Orders:

a. Does each manufacturing order have a unique order number?

_____Yes   _____No

Format_____

b. Does the order number have a significant meaning?

_____Yes   _____No

Format_____

Explanation of meaning_____

_____

c. Is a manufacturing order (pick list) produced?_____

For each stocking level?_____

d. What is the content of manufacturing packet?

____Issues   ____Receipts   ____Pick List (B/M)

____Drawing(s)____Process Sheet____Operating Cards

Other_____

e. Does a shop order cover more than one level of the bill of material? ____Yes ____No

If yes, what?_____

_____

f. Is shop packet produced considering component availability?

____Yes   ____No   If yes, how_____

g. Number of manufacturing orders issued per week?_____

h. Average number of open manufacturing orders?_____

i. Percent of manufacturing orders past due?_____

j. Total hours of past due orders?_____

k. Aging of work orders?_____

9. Lead Times:

Are manufacturing lead times measured?____Yes ____No

Queue____ Wait____ Move____ Set-Up____ Run____

Total cumulative manufacturing lead time typically is _____(weeks) or (months).

Total cumulative manufacturing and purchasing lead time typically is _____(weeks) or (months).

The following describes the elements of the product manufacture cycle:

Assembly: Min_____ Max_____ Typical_____

Fabrication: Min_____ Max_____ Typical_____

Purchasing: Min_____ Max_____ Typical_____

10. How many production planners are there?_____

11. What is the percent of set-up and run time for one unit in relation to total lead time?_____

12. Describe the work center queues.

Nonexistent_____   Low (Minutes)_____

Moderate (Hours)_____   High (Days)_____

Very High (Weeks)_____

13. Does the plant use a Manufacturing Resource Planning System (MRP II)?

____Yes   ____No

If yes, indicate system name and software supplier.

System Name_____

Supplier_____

Developed Internally_____

14. What lot sizing technique is employed in the Material Requirement Planning System for purchased items?_____

_____

15. What lot sizing technique is employed in the Material Requirement Planning System for manufactured items?_____

_____

16. Does the company employ capacity planning techniques?

Rough cut: ____Yes   ____No

How frequently reviewed? _____

Detail Capacity Requirements Planning:
        ____Yes   ____No

How frequently reviewed? _____

Finite: ____Yes   ____No

How frequently reviewed? _____

Is expediting employed on the shop floor?
        ___Yes   ___No

If yes, explain_____

_____

Is de-expediting employed on the shop floor?
        ___Yes ___No

Explain_____

_____

17. Inventory

    a. What types of inventory transactions are presently used?

    ____Receipts ____Issues ____Adjustments

    ____Stock Transfer ____Inspection ____Disposition

    Other_____

    b. Number of inventory transactions per week_____

    c. What inventory reports are produced?

    ____Stock Status ____Transaction Register

    ____Shortage ____Order Status ____ABC

    ____Cycle Count ____ Obsolescence

    Other_____

    d. How are material issues reported?

    ____Issues Transaction ____Pick List ____Automatic

    ____Backflush

18. Inventory Financial Measurement

    ___LIFO ___FIFO ___OSWO ___FISH

    Actual ____   Average ____

DISTRIBUTION AND WAREHOUSING

Distribution and warehousing are often overlooked in the **World Class** arena. We hear so much about **World Class Manufacturing** that we have begun to believe that JIT, TQC and other **World Class** techniques are only for manufacturing folks. This couldn't be further from the truth. Every area of a company needs to address the elimination of waste and to improve their customer relationships. This is because the trend of the future is to ship all products from each manufacturing site directly to the point of *use*. Obviously, distribution and warehousing will play an even more significant role in this future.

Companies such as Digital Equipment Corporation started this process of eliminating waste and improving customer relationships over five years ago. One of the most important issues faced in this process centered around the people in Distribution who were being asked to eliminate their jobs. Other issues were field service and having data from customers accessible to all people in the organization.

This section deals with the concerns which must be addressed in assessing the function of distribution. We have included most of the issues of importance. Each company, depending on the complexity of their distribution function, will add elements it deems necessary.

1. What are the goals and objectives of the company?

    _____

    _____

2. Are policies and procedures identified which will meet customer on-time demands? ____Yes ____No

3. Is there a commitment to attain 100% customer service? ____Yes ____No

4. What inventory control procedures are used to balance multiple stocking locations both within the center and the network?

_____

_____

_____

5. What type of shipping forecasts are provided for each location?

_____

_____

_____

6. Do procedures exist for controlling field returns on a timely basis?

____Yes ____No

7. Are field returns analyzed for cause and effect? ____Yes ____No

    If yes, how?

_____

_____

_____

8. Describe how warehouse space requirements are determined:

_____

_____

_____

9. In multi-warehouse distribution environments, is there a policy to govern choice of location?   ____Yes   ____No

10. What modes of distribution are used and how are they chosen?

_____

_____

_____

11. How are distribution routes selected and managed?

_____

_____

_____

12. What type of procedure is used for stock location?

_____

_____

_____

13. Is there a sequence to optimize manpower utilization and truck loading sequence? ____Yes ____No

14. Are goods pre-staged? ____Yes ____No

15. How are work assignments made for the distribution people?

_____

_____

_____

16. What type of quality audit is performed prior to shipment?

_____

_____

_____

17. Describe the method for inventory cycle count:

_____

_____

_____

18. Is there a procedure to correct the cause of inventory errors?

____Yes ____No

19. What is the company's approach to solving problems?

_____

_____

_____

20. What is the frequency of reporting performance to management?

_____

_____

_____

21. Does reporting compare overall and short-range plans vs. actuals by the following indices?

    a) Number of people____
    b) Manhours worked____
    c) Productivity or performance percentage____
    d) Plan vs. actual____
    e) Overtime____
    f) On-time delivery____
    g) Truckload capacity and utilization____
    h) Schedule attainment____
    i) Key backlog status____
    j) Order status____

22. How are customer back orders controlled?

_____

_____

23. What method is used for prioritizing customer back orders?

_____

_____

_____

24. Is there a procedure for optimizing routings, zones, vehicle routes to minimize backtracking, duplication and route criss-crossing? ____Yes ____No

    Describe:

_____

_____

_____

CHAPTER SEVEN

Supply
Base
Management

At a time when costs related to purchasing account for over 50% of the total cost of a product, it is necessary to pay attention to the supply base management role in a company. Paying attention is vital when one considers the effects of domestic and global competition.

Procurement's role has become increasingly important as companies finally realize and discover the impact of cost today. There is an urgent need to rethink the way one conducts the business of procurement. Companies must make the transition from Purchasing as a department of clerical paper-shufflers to Purchasing as a department involved in the planning, marketing, design, engineering, production and quality control functions of a company in order to attain **World Class Status**. Our book, **Just-In-Time Purchasing:** *In Pursuit of Excellence*, addresses this subject in complete detail.

WHAT IS JUST-IN-TIME PURCHASING?

<u>**Just-In-Time Purchasing**</u> <u>is the uninterrupted flow</u>
<u>of 100% acceptable materials delivered</u>
<u>at optimal cost, 100% on time.</u>

American and foreign companies must subscribe to the definition above if they want to enjoy the lower costs and increased profits which ensue. And if your competition is not embarking on a **Just-In-Time Purchasing** program, you can be sure that they will be very shortly. It is too costly *not* to begin.

We deem the following as critical: Supplier Partnerships, Total Cost and Total Quality Control. These are the foundation which will support the entire structure.

1. <u>Supplier Partnerships</u>. In **Just-In-Time Purchasing**, it is far more profitable and reliable to develop long-term relationships with suppliers in which they are partners, not victims. This necessitates a high level of trust and cooperation not usually found in today's business world. Long-term partnerships only work in two directions. If a supplier is shipping "zero-defect" material, he expects to receive production schedules from your company which will help him in meeting your needs in a timely fashion and payment per the terms of the agreement. If he doesn't get your co-operation, he cannot maintain the quality standards you demand. Partnership comes into being with the implementation of a Sup-

plier Certification program (as explained in our book, **Supplier Certification:** *Achieving Excellence*) which seeks to educate and train suppliers in the necessity and virtues of process and quality controls in their facilities. The result must be "win-win."

2. <u>Total Cost Approach</u>. A prevailing thought today is that we must raise the selling price of products in order to maintain profits while costs rise. Unfortunately, this can lead to a never-ending spiral upwards. When I increase my price, your costs go up. So, you raise your price and eventually that makes my cost go up and so on. **World Class Companies**, however, take this equation and look at it in another way.

Instead of constantly revising selling prices upward, we begin by value analyzing all of the costs associated with the product. The objective is to base the selling price based on total cost and a fair profit. We keep the selling price and profit the same by attacking and reducing all the cost elements.

Many companies have successfully implemented supplier-driven value analysis efforts as part of their partnership relations. This allows for a sharing of the savings on improvements recommended by the supplier. It truly maximizes the win/win approach and financially rewards both customer and supplier. The suppliers are motivated by the ability to increase their profits immediately and customers by an immediate reduction in costs.

Total costs are those costs incurred by the whole company in manufacturing a product. Some of these costs are apparent and some are hidden. Current accounting methods tend to depend on price analysis which uses the seller's price without examining the separate elements of cost and profit within functions.

3. Total Quality Control. Purchasing plays a lead role in this area. Many of the factors which influence quality at supplier's facility, such as lead time, set-up reduction, Statistical Quality Control, Supplier Certification Programs and supplier "zero-defect" programs, are now the responsibility of Purchasing. This is because purchasing is responsible for supplying the right material, at the right time, in the right place, in the right quantity, every time. This puts a premium on making sure that the material is always free of defects. The **World Class Environment** functions with only 100% quality components. Purchasing has the responsibility to implement a quality control program with each supplier.

Purchasing must act in concert with all departments. Supplier Partnerships, the Total Cost Approach and Total Quality Control are the building blocks of **World Class Status**. Here is a questionnaire to help you make a preliminary assessment of your purchasing functions.

PURCHASING POLICY

1. Does a purchasing policy manual exist? ____Yes ____No

2. What is the company's statement regarding conflict of interest and gifts?
    _____
    _____
    _____

3. List purchasing objectives:

    a) Profit improvement____
    b) Inventory levels____
    c) Service (shortage) levels____
    d) Quality____
    e) Price____

4. What is the policy on the development of sources?

   _____Single _____Sole _____Multiple

5. Does a procedure exist for approving purchase orders?

   _____Yes _____No

6. Describe the signature level authority for:

   Buyer:_____

   Sr. Buyer:_____

   Supervisor:_____

   Manager:_____

   Director:_____

   Vice President:_____

7. What limitations are placed on the value of single purchase orders?

   _____
   _____
   _____

8. Are the following responsibilities defined?

   a) Expediting delivery_____
   b) Supplier selection and approval_____
   c) Specification control and communication_____

9. What departments does purchasing support in addition to production?

   _____
   _____
   _____

10. Does any other function place purchase orders with suppliers?

    ____Yes ____No

11. Is a cash flow analysis provided? ____Yes ____No

12. Is an expedite/de-expedite list provided for?

    a) Shortage items only?   ____Yes ____No
    b) Overdue items?   ____Yes ____No
    c) Due now, next week, etc.? ____Yes ____No

13. Are purchase contracts issued in addition to individual purchase orders?
    ____Yes ____No

PURCHASING OPERATIONS

1. How are purchase orders prepared? ____Manual
    ____Computer ____EDI

2. Are prenumbered purchase orders utilized?_____

    a. What is the size/format of PO number?_____

3. Are multiple items allowed on a PO?_____

    a. Are they identified with a line number?_____

4. How are multiple deliveries documented on the PO?_____

_____

5. Is a purchase requisition submitted to purchasing?

    ____Yes   ____No   From what function:_____

a. What data is present on the requisition?

_____Item Number _____Quantity _____Date Required

Other_____

6. Are blanket purchase orders utilized?_____

a. For a single supplier?_____

b. Is a release notice sent to supplier?_____

c. What information is on the release notice?_____

_____

7. Are systems contracts utilized? _____Yes _____No

What items are included?_____

_____

8. Are suppliers identified by unique number?_____

9. Where is supplier data kept? _____

10. Are suppliers identified for all items? ___Yes ___No

11. Is the supplier's part number utilized?_____

a. Maximum number of characters and format:_____

_____

12. What information is maintained by item for a supplier?

_____

13. Is copy of PO used to authorize receipts? ____Yes ____No

    If no, how is authorization given?_____

    _____

14. Are partial receipts allowed?_____

    a. How documented?_____

15. Is receiving centralized?_____

16. Is count verified at receiving?_____

17. Is inspection performed?_____

    a. How is disposition of rejected material reported?

    _____

18. Are buyers assigned by item?_____

    Commodity?_____

19. What reports are produced for purchasing?

    ____Open Order Status ____Past Due Receipts

    ____Daily Receipts ____Open Orders by Supplier

    ____Supplier List   Other_____

20. Number of purchase orders issued per month?_____

    a. Average number of open PO's_____

    b. Average number of line items per PO_____

21. Is purchase unit of measure same as stocking unit of measure? _____

    a. How are exceptions handled?_____

    _____

22. How often are all of the positions in the purchasing function reviewed from a time management perspective? _____

23. Percent of purchase orders past due?_____

24. Are supplier purchased lead times measured actual vs. stated?

    ____Yes   ____No

    If yes, what percent of orders are expedited?_____
    What percent of orders are de-expedited?_____

25. How are purchase requirements determined?

    E.O.Q.   _____
    Lot Size   _____
    Fixed Period   _____
    Fixed Quantity   _____
    Blanket Orders   _____

26. Is there an Approved Supplier List?   ___Yes ___No

    Is there a Qualified Supplier List?   ___Yes ___No

    Is there a Certified Supplier List?   ___Yes ___No

27. Is there a supplier certification program?

    ____Yes   ____No

        Percent of suppliers certified?_____
    Number if part numbers certified?_____

28. Has a supplier symposium been conducted?

____Yes   ____No

If yes, explain_____

_____

_____

_____

29. Are the purchasing professionals performance reviews directly related to performance of the suppliers they manage?

____Yes   _____No

30. How many suppliers are presently shipping their product:

To stock____# _____% To W.I.P.____# _____%

31. Has there been a concentrated supplier reduction effort?
___Yes   ____No

If yes, how many have been reduced?_____
    Total number of current suppliers?_____

32. The percentage of purchased material cost to total manufacturing cost is?
<40%____41%-50%___51%-60%____61%-70%____>70%___

33. Is there a philosophy for where suppliers must be located?
___Yes ___No

If yes, what is the philosophy objective?_____

_____

34. What has been the contribution to your company's profit from purchasing during the last five years? _____

35. How is purchasing organized? (Attach organization chart)

_____

_____

_____

36. Does your company employ the buyer/planner concept?

___Yes ___No

37. Is purchased price variance measured? ___Yes ___No

38. Is a formal cost model being used by purchasing to evaluate suppliers? ___Yes ___No

39. How many suppliers are on file?_____

Number active in the last 12 months?_____

Are supplier numbers assigned?_____

40. Is supplier history maintained by part?_____Price?_____

Performance to due date?_____Quality?_____

Total purchases?_____

41. How are suppliers selected and developed?_____

_____

42. What is the supplier sourcing philosophy of the company?

Single____ Multiple____ Sole____

43. Is a formal supplier rating system being used to evaluate a supplier's total performance? ___Yes ___No

44. How is RMA (Return Material Authority) processed?

    _____

    _____

    _____

45. What percent of purchase orders placed are approved at the
    Director/Vice President level? _____

    How many purchasing orders don't get approved at the
    Director/Vice President level? _____

CHAPTER EIGHT

Total
Cost

PRODUCT COSTING

With **World Class Status** comes the adoption of and conversion to a Total Cost Approach. A supplier's quoted price (or the manufacturing cost) is not the true cost. Quality and delivery must also be taken into account, but this will mean getting Finance to look beyond the traditional cost systems. We can no longer be dependent upon price analysis as the only criterion for determining total product costs. Cost analysis, on the other hand, examines all the costs involved in getting a product to market.

Many companies' cost accounting systems are not producing the results that support the progress toward achieving World Class Status. They provide managers with incorrect product cost information which adds pressure on dealings with suppliers, manufacturers and customers. Strategies become suspect when decisions are based on faulty information.

An effective cost signal sends out many different signals which need to be identified and corrected. The total cost approach demands financial involvement which goes beyond the traditional results and which seeks out these signals. Enhancement begins with asking the proper questions which establish the need for different results.

Here are some of the questions a company should be asking itself:

What does it cost

> **— for materials to sit?**
> **— to miss a delivery?**
> **— to process engineering changes?**
> **— for a machine to break down?**
> **— for a kit to be short?**
> **— to run manufacturing operations?**

A true test of your accounting system is whether you have the answers to these questions. We suggest that you ask these questions throughout the organization. If an operator knows how much it costs for a machine to break down, then you can be sure that you have a system which makes information available in order to resolve issues. This is a cost system's most significant contribution to achieving World Class Status.

COST IMPROVEMENT

In order to achieve success with this method, it will be necessary for you to revamp the cost accounting system and incorporate life cycle accounting which supports World Class improvement efforts. The key element in long-term cost improvement is the analysis of all costs associated with the manufacturing of a product to reach the market.

These cost elements represent all activities performed within the company. Cost improvement cannot be restricted to the shop floor. Finance needs to look for other areas of opportunity. We encourage clients to start with an analysis of cost which begins with a product design. Cost should then be tracked through marketing and sales, procurement of raw material and components, the production process and shipping and distribution activities. No area should be exempt from the cost improvement effort.

Cost improvement is a many-lapped race, perhaps like the Indianapolis 500, but more like a sports car rally. In a rally, drivers must arrive at designated checkpoints at certain times. Winners are those racers who most closely follow the rally's instructions. Not only does this mean pinpoint timing, but accurate routing. The same can apply to a company on the course of cost improvement. Your navigator, or controller, must help you stay on route so that you will arrive on time with the right product that satisfies customer requirements and at the lowest total cost.

Driving cost improvement throughout the organization will require an improved cost reporting system. Elements of cost need to be added to the General Ledger in order to expand their visibility. We recommend establishing the following categories of cost which support World Class activities:

WORLD CLASS COST CATEGORIES

Cost of Quality
Cost of Inventory
Cost of Processing
Cost of Maintenance
Cost of Production
Cost of Support

Included in these categories would be the actual cost elements which need to be collected and reported in order to reflect improvements.

Cost systems will get a lot of attention in the next ten years, and just like other World Class activities, they must be viewed as a continuous improvement process. A review of the cost function will show you how innovative or how traditional they are. Keep in mind that most cost systems which are used today were developed in 1905. Why, in light of that information, do we continue to look for cost reduction in the direct labor area of cost? The problem we face is that current financial systems are developed by software people who still view accounting in traditional ways. These software packages continue to force us to adopt traditional practices. The trend will be for finance people to develop their own tools.

I can remember having a debate with Steve Jobs about controlling cost at the Macintosh factory. He wanted twelve cost points. I wanted one. Why would we want to control that many elements of cost when we build a unit every 27 seconds? The requirement here was to simplify the cost process.

Let's review some of the issues facing the cost area:

1. Is a standard cost system presently utilized?_____

    Other_____

2. Is system computerized? ____Yes ____No

Are costs developed?_____ Estimated? _____

Allocated? _____

3. Is the bill of material, utilized by manufacturing, used to develop cost?

_____Yes   _____No

If no, what is used for cost development?_____

_____

4. Are routings utilized to develop labor cost?   ___Yes   ___No

If no, what is used?_____

5. Is set up cost considered in standard cost?   ___Yes   ___No

   a. If yes, how is it calculated?

   _____Hours x Labor Rate   _____Fixed Rate

   Other_____

   b. If labor rate, is a separate set up rate utilized?_____

   _____By Work Center   _____By Labor Grade

6. How are labor dollars calculated?_____

_____

a. If labor rate is utilized, are rates identified by:

____Work Center ____Labor Grade

____Employee   ____Work Cell

Other_____

7. Cost Maintenance:

a. What cost types are maintained?

____Standard (Frozen) ____Standard (Current)

____Engineering Other_____

b. What cost elements are maintained at the component level?
   (i.e. labor, burden, material)

1. _____ 2. _____ 3. _____

4. _____ 5. _____ 6. _____

7. _____ 8. _____ 9. _____

c. What cost elements are rolled up and maintained at the assembly level?

1. _____ 2. _____ 3. _____

4. _____ 5. _____ 6. _____

7. _____ 8. _____ 9. _____

d. What cost elements are displayed on reports?

Inventory Reports:_____

_____

Cost Accounting Reports:_____

_____

What cost reports are presently utilized?
1._____
2._____
3._____
4._____
5._____
6._____
7._____

e. How often are costs updated?_____

At time of updating are all BOM levels updated?

____Yes   ____No

If no, explain:_____

_____

8. How is burden applied?____% Labor $ ____% Material $

____Rate Against Labor Hours ____Fixed Amount

____Variable By Contract _____Other

9. Are direct costing reports available for:

	Yes	No
Plants	_____	_____
Cost Centers	_____	_____
Processes	_____	_____
Products	_____	_____
Work Orders	_____	_____
Repetitive Process	_____	_____

10. Is Inventory carrying cost calculated? ___Yes ___No

    If yes, what rate is used monthly, and how is it calculated?

    _____

    _____

11. How is inventory valued?_____

    _____

    _____

12. Are any non-financial cost elements collected?

    ____Yes ____No

    How are non-financial costs calculated and used?

    _____

    _____

    _____

13. Do operating reports reflect the cost of non-conformance?

    ____Yes ____No

14. Do reports distinguish between value added and non-value added cost?

    ____Yes ____No

15. How is non-value added cost used to support cost reduction?

    _____

    _____

    _____

    _____

16. How is work-in-process inventory calculated?

    _____

    _____

    _____

17. Is life cycle accounting being considered in finance results?

    ____Yes ____No

18. Is the cost of quality collected by category:

    ____Appraisal costs?

    ____Failure costs?

    ____Preventive costs?

GENERAL LEDGER

To achieve **World Class Status** will require a company to streamline the General Ledger process. All too often, when it comes to building a network with the Finance function, people forget about common goals. Suddenly, it is not the team, but "us" against "them." All Finance seems to do today is tell us what we can't do and build fences of financial restraints to make us feel penned in.

"If only they understood!" is the constant lament.

Finance needs to be involved early in your movement toward **World Class Excellence**. Forming this link with Finance is as much everybody's responsibility as it is Finance's. It is even more important in **World Class Manufacturing** where the old methods of financial accounting must be replaced.

Companies who measure themselves with traditional yardsticks will have a difficult time justifying the **World Class** process and resulting savings. It is no wonder we are besieged by traditional constraints which affect performance measurement and correct decision-making.

Traditional General Ledger models are primarily formatted to produce financial results for external purposes. These external purposes will not disappear in the World Class environment. However, the type of results that we are looking for internally have been captured in aggregate totals buried in the General Ledger. World Class companies are recognizing the value of segregating this data in order to measure total cost and thus run the organization more efficiently and cost effectively.

The General Ledger will require more account numbers which reflect the performance of all functions within the organization. As companies realize the importance of controlling the components of overhead, we will start to see more internal accounts which promote cost improvement in World Class operations.

World Class systems should provide companies with new cost categories that distinguish between value added and non-value added costs. This break down will support opportunities to involve everyone in cost reduction.

The question then arises as to how cost can be captured, reported and distributed within the organization. World Class systems should provide finance with cost allocation that allows for data from the General Ledger to be split off and collected into categories which reflect performance areas we are trying to improve. The next step is to spread the collected cost back to responsibility levels which can be reported and measured. This "split and spread" activity can be accomplished with various statistics which are used to assist in the calculation process. These statistics can include head counts, square footage, transactions and dollars.

The information gathered in this section will work to stimulate your brain to view this function differently. Be advised that you should not study a process to death. You will never make a decision this way. Follow the advice given to me by a good friend: "If it feels good, do it."

1. How many account numbers in Chart Of Accounts? _____

    What is the format? _____

    Is there significance? _____

    Are there interfaces to other accounting systems?_____

2. When does the financial year end? _____

    How many periods are there? _____

3. How long does it take to produce period end reports? _____

    How long does it take to produce year end reports? _____

    What additional processes are required at year end? _____

4. Is there a formal budgeting process? _____

    Cash budget? _____ Capital budget? _____

5. Is the budget used to control expenses at the department level?

    _____

6. How many people are primarily involved with:

    ACCOUNTING FUNCTION   NO. OF PEOPLE

        General Accounting   _____
        Cost Accounting   _____
        Accounts Payable   _____
        Accounts Receivable   _____
        Controller   _____
        Payroll   _____
        Treasurer   _____
        Other   _____

7. How are indirect costs allocated? _____

8. What financial reports are currently being prepared?

    _____

9. Define the opportunities in the Financial area for improvement:

_____

_____

_____

_____

10. Does all data flow to the General Ledger?

_____Yes   _____No

11. How is justification of cost taking place today?

_____

_____

_____

_____

_____

12. How are performance measurements extracted from the General Ledger?

_____

_____

_____

_____

13. Does the system include an allocation process to develop cost elements using any of the following?

Splits:

By product_____

By work cell_____

By department_____

Spreads:

Percent_____

Weighted average_____

Other calculation_____

Statistics:

Head count_____

Square footage_____

Transactions_____

Other (name)_____

_____

_____

14. Is data from the General Ledger used for performance measurements?

____Yes   ____No

If yes, list:

_____

_____

_____

_____

JIT DELIVERY TO JIT PAYMENT

World Class Excellence will mean connecting *JIT delivery to JIT payment*. This will not only improve supplier relations, but eliminate much paperwork for Finance. This double-sided benefit is not possible until a company can convince Finance to eliminate invoices for every shipment, especially if they are daily. Finance may look at a JIT payment schedule and see not less paperwork, but decidedly more. But, in a company which has achieved **World Class Status**, it is possible to eliminate matching invoices because it has guaranteed daily shipment of quality parts through a Supplier Certification program. Such a company will soon know if a shipment was received. Its production line will not shut down. You don't need an invoice to tell you that.

Bar coding applications should have Finance staff involvement in order to obtain the desired results. A Japanese company successfully receives 2,000 different components a day with the use of bar coding technology in Receiving and Accounts Payable.

If having your line shut down sounds like a frightening way to have financial accountability, don't panic. Remember, a **World Class Company** has built a bridge of trust with its suppliers. It has checked their financial status, their delivery reliability, their quality and it has monitored each of these areas. It has created a strong structure which will eliminate wasteful or redundant paperwork by working with Finance in a partnership.

A **World Class Company** can strengthen this bridge of trust even more by paying suppliers quickly. Daily payment is, of course, an ideal (which, incidentally, can be greatly helped along by bar coding and EDI). But daily payment is not the only solution. If the typical wait for payment is 60 days, reward good suppliers by cutting it to 30 days; if it's 30, cut it to 15. The point is that no suppliers in their right mind want to jeopardize a win/win situation. Companies must understand that a **World Class Business** looks at Accounts Payable from a total cost approach. If a company loses a month of interest because it paid more quickly, then consider how much more money it will have saved by quickly shipping to its customer and by lowering its inventory cost. The issue is to pay on time for on time delivery of products. This will be a major change for most companies.

1. Are the same A/P methods used for non-production material (i.e., supplies) as for production materials? _____

     Explain: _____

     _____

2. Are invoices matched against receipts and purchase orders?

     _____

3. Are cash requirements forecasted for future periods? _____

4. Is there a method used to take advantage of supplier discounts?

    Explain: _____

_____

5. How often are A/P invoices paid? _____

6. How are special checks handled?

    COD_____

    Manual_____

    Prepayment_____

7. Is there a detailed check voucher for each check? _____

8. Are checks pre-numbered? _____

9. How is reconciliation of paid checks handled? _____

_____

10. How are returns to suppliers handled? _____

11. Is there an adequate method of security on confidential supplier information?_____

    Explain:_____

_____

12. Flow today's A/P process from receipt through check payment.

_____

_____

13. How are the following application used or planned in A/P?

Bar Coding?_____

_____

_____

Kanban?_____

_____

_____

EDI?_____

_____

_____

14. How are the costs of administering A/P collected?

Overhead?_____

Allocation to product?_____

15. What is the average age of the A/P function?
_____ 0-30 _____ 31-60 _____ 61-90 _____ 91>

16. Define areas of opportunity.

_____

_____

_____

ACCOUNTS RECEIVABLE

As in the area of Accounts Payable, we must work with our customers to pay on a Just-In-Time basis. A partnership at the customer level is necessary if we are to make what each customer wants quickly. In addition, the trend is toward limiting the number of customers that a company has, just as companies are reducing the number of suppliers.

Application of EDI, bar coding and various new methods will require our financial people to work with customers in the future. World Class involvement means cleaning up the paper process as well.

1. How many customers are on file?_____

   Number active in last 12 months?_____

   Are customer numbers assigned?_____

2. Is customer history maintained by product?_____

   Service parts?_____ Total sales dollars?_____

   Other_____

3. How is credit worthiness determined, maintained, and

   communicated?_____

   _____

4. Is there an adequate method of security on confidential customer information?_____

   Explain:_____

5. How often are invoices prepared?_____

   Are they prenumbered?_____

6. How are special invoices handled?_____

7. How are customer returns handled?_____

8. How often is cash applied?_____

9. How often are receivables aged?_____

   Is a trial balance prepared?_____

10. What are average outstanding A/R balances?

    Current   _____   Over 90 _____

    Over 30 _____   Over 120 _____

    Over 60 _____

11. Where are standard discount terms?_____

CHAPTER NINE

Operations

World Class Status can be achieved by all manufacturing companies, whether they are Repetitive, Discrete/Job Shop, or Process/Continuous Flow.

A *repetitive* manufacturer is a company in which the production of discrete units are planned and executed via a daily production schedule. Material flows sequentially, based on customer demand as it is pulled through the shop.

A *discrete/job shop* manufacturer is an organization in which departments or work centers are organized around particular types of equipment or operations, such as drilling, forging, spinning or assembling. These companies will move toward group technology in the future in order to compete effectively. In order to survive, job shops also have to move toward a Just-In-Time environment in which customer satisfaction is job number one.

A *process/continuous flow* manufacturer has a production system in which the production equipment is organized and sequenced according to the steps involved in producing the product. The term denotes that material flow is continuous during the production process and that the routings of jobs are fixed. The major issue for these companies will be product changeovers and set-up reduction.

FLEXIBLE MANUFACTURING

World Class Companies will need to adopt *flexible manufacturing*. Flexible manufacturers are capable of responding or conforming to changes in demand in the manufacturing environment. They must be capable of quick turnaround and little, if any, set-up time. Flexible manufacturing moves us away from relying upon the accuracy of long-range forecasting by Marketing to relying on a daily schedule based on customer demand. This transition will not be easy.

Below are five major strategies to pursue in order to become a **World Class** manufacturer:

<u>ORGANIZING</u>
<u>FOR</u>
<u>WORLD CLASS STATUS</u>

- **Educate all people about WORLD CLASS objectives in order to form a strong foundation and establish objectives.**

- **Create ownership by delegating authority and responsibility to the operator.**

- **Provide a proven process that can be easily implemented and accepted.**

- **Establish measurements which illustrate the success of a program and the opportunities for continuous improvement.**

- **Press for results—challenge people.**

- **Do not be satisfied with early results.**

Maintaining control over our companies requires us to look at traditional methods of integrating operations in a new light. The purpose of this book is not to redefine Just-In-Time (JIT). JIT is already a redefinition and review of all the areas which are key to **World Class Status**. We have been witness to many companies which have no manufacturing goals or objectives at all. How can this happen!? American companies have concentrated on people for years while overlooking tooling, testing, equipment processes and quality.

This chapter defines the review process necessary for your operations. Understanding a business today is important to providing a direction for the future. Today is the baseline. As improvements are made, that base will change daily.

1. Describe the nature of the facility.

    Process_____ % Repetitive_____ %

    Discrete_____ % Combination_____ %

2. What present methods are used in job scheduling and loading?

   _____

   _____

   _____

3. Are any orders released without component availability?

   ____Yes ____No

4. How are production priorities established?

   _____

   _____

   _____

5. Labor is reported? ____By Job ____By Item

   Other_____

6. Who reports labor? ____Worker ____Supervisors

   Other_____

7. What is the method of labor reporting? ____Data Collection

   ____Time Card   Other_____

8. Employees clock____on____off all production jobs?

9. Are pieces counted? ____Yes ____No

   Exceptions_____

10. Are piece counts verified?_____ By whom?_____

11. Is material movement reported by operation?
    _____Yes _____No   Other_____

12. Is scrap reported by operation? _____Yes _____No

    Other_____

13. Is set-up reported separate from run time? _____Yes _____No

    Comments_____

    _____

14. Is labor reporting used for payroll? _____Yes _____No

15. Basis for payroll: _____Hourly _____Incentive

    Other_____

16. Is there a dispatch center? _____Yes _____No

    A. Describe the dispatch function: _____

    _____

    B. Does a schedule release procedure exist?

        _____Yes _____No

17. Is a shop traveler used? _____Yes _____No

    Contents: _____Operation Cards _____Process Sheet

    _____Send/Receive Transactions _____Scrap Transactions

    Other_____

18. Production order and related shop paper contain the following dates:

_____Date Generated _____Start Date _____Complete Date

Other_____

19. What is the basis and policy for scheduling work at a work center?_____

20. Priority is determined by:

_____Start Date _____Complete Date _____Contract Priority

Other_____

21. How are alternate operations handled?_____

_____

22. Who decides when an alternate is used? _____Foreman

_____Dispatch _____Planner _____Operator _____Customer

Other_____

23. Labor performance reporting is reported by: _____Employee

_____Work Center _____Job Other_____

24. Describe the present method of capacity planning:

_____

_____

_____

25. What feedback exists when short-term capacity constraints exist?

_____

_____

_____

26. Capacity Reports:

A. Are capacity reports produced for:

____Long Range ____Short Range

B. Do they contain: ____Released ____Firm ____Planned Orders

C. Is detail presented by operation? ____Yes ____No

D. Is detail regenerated based on MRP? ____Yes ____No

E. How are capacity/load reports used?_____

_____

_____

F. How does load leveling take place? _____

_____

_____

G. What percent, on average, of the theoretical maximum capacity is scheduled? ____%

H. Is there a facility rationalization plan to eliminate wasted space and improve facility utilization? ____Yes ____No

27. Is quality visible on the shop floor?   ____Yes   ____No

    Explain_____

    _____

28. How much material handling is required to support production?

    ____None   ____Minimal   ____Moderate   ____High

29. What is the direct labor component of the manufacturing cost?

    Low (High Automation)_____

    Moderate (Some Automation)_____

    High (Manual)_____

    Indicate percentage of direct labor cost to total manufacturing cost_____%.

30. The life cycle of products is? Low_____ Medium_____ High_____

31. Are the bottleneck areas in the production process stationary, or do they move?

    Where?_____

    When?_____

32. How long does it take to process an engineering change notice?

    <24 Hours_____ 5 Days_____ 1 Month_____ > 2 Months_____

33. What percent of the operators are crosstrained?_____

34. Is Bar Coding being employed in the business?
_____Yes _____No

If yes, what areas presently utilize Bar Coding?_____

_____

35. Are bottlenecks clearly identified and used to focus Manufac-turing Resource Planning?   _____Yes   _____No

36. Are there any islands of automation being utilized today?

_____Yes   _____No

Are set-ups broken down to produce priority items?

_____Yes _____No

37. Are the following variances captured and reported?

Material Usage   _____Yes _____No

Purchase Price   _____Yes _____No

Labor   _____Yes _____No

Overhead   _____Yes _____No

38. To what extent has throughput been increased as a result of JIT initiatives?

<10%____11%-40%____ 41%-80%____ 81%-95%____ >95%____

39. To what extent have setups been reduced as a result of JIT efforts?

<10%____ 11%-40%____ 41%-80%____ 81%-94%____ >95%____

40. To what extent has Work-In-Process been reduced by JIT efforts?

    <10%____ 11%-40%____ 41%-80%____ 80%-94%____ >95%____

    Finished goods, raw material.

    <10%____ 11%-40%____ 41%-80%____ 80%-94%____ >95%____

41. How is On-Time Delivery measured to the delivery date?

    (+/-) Hours____   One Day____   Five Days____
    Other_____

42. What major areas of opportunity have surfaced in the Manu-facturing area by direct labor?

    _____

    _____

    _____

43. When an overload condition exists, describe the method to adjust the master schedule:

    _____

    _____

    _____

44. What policy exists to disposition any scrap on the production floor?

    _____

    _____

    _____

45. Is there adherence to releasing schedules on orders to customer demand? ____Yes ____No

46. Is GMP (Good Manufacturing Practices) adhered to?
____Yes ____No

47. Describe the overall appearance of each plant which has been reviewed:

Plant 1

_____

_____

_____

Plant 2

_____

_____

_____

Plant 3

_____

_____

_____

48. Is the current period of the master schedule overstated due to overdue orders? ____Yes ____No

49. Are there periods of excessive overtime and idle capacity?
____Yes ____No

PROCESS AND ROUTING

Shop routings are the basic plan for the manufacturing of a particular item. They answer three questions:

1. Where are the items produced?
2. What must be done to produce the items and with what tools?
3. How long does it take to produce the items?

Traditionally, there is a primary and alternate routing. Alternate routings come into use when capacity overages or machine breakdowns occur. The result is poor quality and lack of process control. Primary routings are the most efficient, reliable and least costly. A **World Class Manufacturer** has the responsibility of making sure that the process stays under control at all times. A **World Class Manufacturer** also has responsibility for seeing that processes are under control in a supplier's plant.

1. Have routings been identified for each manufactured item?

    _____

2. How are routings maintained? _____ Manual _____ Computer

    Who maintains the routings? _____

3. What information is maintained for each routing?

    _____ Set Up Hours _____ Run Hours _____ Description
    _____ Work Center _____ Tools _____ Labor Grade
    _____ Operation Number _____ Other

4. What is the size and format of:
   Set Up Hours _____ Run Hours _____
   Move/Queue Hours _____

5. Are routings identified for:
   _____ Outside Processing _____ Alternative Routings

6. What is the size and format of operation number?
   Format _____

7. If alternate routings are used, are controls in place to insure a quality product? _____Yes _____No

8. What is the size for work center identification?
   Format _____

9. Has queue/move time been established? _____

   _____ By Operation _____ By Work Center

10. What information is maintained by the work center?

    _____ Description _____ Shifts _____ Machines
    _____ Number of People _____ Other

11. How are changes to routings controlled?
    _____ Revision Letter _____ Effectivity Date _____ Other

12. What is the basis for standards?
    _____ Time Study _____ Adjusted Actual _____ Estimated
    _____ Other

13. Number of items with routings? _____

    Average number of operations/routings? _____

14. Is the manufacturing process under Statistical Process Control? _____Yes _____No

15. Explain the use of alternate routings or processes:

_____

_____

_____

16. Is SPC employed on the factory floor? _____Yes _____No

17. Are process sheets under Engineering Change Control?

_____Yes _____No

18. Are work center loads reviewed against planned order requirements and capacity? _____Yes _____No

SET-UP REDUCTION

Set-up reduction is one part of a large assortment of activities which will prepare your company for **World Class Status**. The benefits which can be derived from a set-up reduction program inside of a TBC environment will not only prepare the company for the future, but will help you to fund that future. The benefits below can make any set-up program self-funding:

- Lower cost of parts and assemblies produced — a result of better relations with customers, lower inventory costs, better coordination between manu-facturing and design, production and planning.

- Greatly improved quality — lower cost of quality or non-conformance with delivery of zero-defect material.

- Improved design and producibility — new products are not designed behind closed doors and then thrown over walls to the production facility. The Design team works with suppliers and production people to design tooling for quick changeovers at the start of the design process.

- Improved administrative efficiency — as paperwork diminishes and scheduling improves, the result is better administrative coordination.

- Increased capacity — in terms of the shop floor, better utilization of material, faster set-up, reduced lead times, and elimination of waste.

- Inventory reduction — measured by a comparable reduction in set-up times and lot sizes.

- Lot size reduction — results in small lots being produced daily. Finally, we can avoid using the Economic Order Quantity (EOQ) and convert to lot-for-lot.

MEETING THE COMPETITION

Set-up reduction will play a large role in funding your company's future. A very large role. Companies will need to meet the competition by:

- Increasing capital turnover.
- Freeing up storage space for manufacturing use.
- Reducing stock-handling operations.

- Performing mixed production.
- Shipping on time, 100 percent of the time to customers.

Machine work rates will improve and productive capacity will expand. As set-ups become quicker and easier, the number of set-up errors will disappear and consequently the number of defective goods diminishes. Also, the need for special set-up skills will be eliminated. Both safety and tool management improve as well. In short, set-up reduction can shorten production times to the point where changes in demand can be responded to immediately by only making the quantity your customer wants.

We believe that set-up reduction supports the movement toward **World Class Status** by simplifying production processes and eliminating the wasteful element of lead time — set-up time. Companies have a lot to gain in this area which is why we isolated it as a major section. Jerry Claunch and Phil Stang's book, **Set-Up Reduction:** *Saving Dollars with Common Sense*, (PT Publications) combines theory with practical, hands-on applications to assist companies with this critical element of **World Class Manufacturing**.

1. Are there teams organized for the purpose of reducing the time to set up work centers?

<u>Internal</u>   <u>External</u>

____Yes ____No   ____Yes ____No

If yes, how many teams are there?

1_____   2-3_____   3-4_____   >4_____

2. As set up time is reduced, is there effective communication, including a standard procedure, to reduce lot sizes?
   ____Yes ____No

   If yes, how much have lot sizes been reduced?

   50%____ 75%____ 90%____

3. Have set up reduction techniques been applied throughout?

   ____Yes ____No

4. Is there a procedure established for set up reduction?

   ____Yes ____No

   If yes, does procedure include:

   ____Video Tapes

   ____Video Analysis Documentation

   ____Internal vs. External Separation

   ____Tooling Checklists

   ____Documented method and procedures for each set up

   ____Tooling repair work order

   ____Tool Storage close to point of use

   ____Periodic review of videotapes to exploit "new" techniques and equipment

5. Does Set Up Reduction team review new tool designs prior to manufacture?

   ____Yes ____No

If no, does tool design follow guidelines of set up reduction?

____Yes   ____No

6. Has a Set Up Training Course been conducted?

____Yes ____No

7. Describe the areas where Set-Up Reduction can have an immediate impact:

_____

_____

_____

_____

_____

_____

_____

8. List all areas and examples where the company has applied Set-Up Reduction.

_____

_____

_____

_____

_____

9. What effect will Set-Up reduction have on Inventory Reduction?

_____

_____

10. Do the operators conduct any Set-Up as part of the operation?

____Yes ____No

11. What method is used to document a set-up procedure?

_____

_____

_____

12. Are performance measurements and continuous improvement goals established for set-up reduction?

____Yes ____No

13. Are widely visible graphic displays of perfomance in use?

____Yes ____No

Where?_____

_____

_____

ZERO BREAKDOWN MAINTENANCE

Preventive maintenance is crucial to the success or failure of achieving **World Class Status**. Zero breakdown maintenance basically insures that any equipment used in the manufacturing of a product will be in full operating condition each and every time it needs to be used. The responsibility of a Maintenance team is to uncover and solve problems *before* they interfere with production. Its goal is to be proactive, instead of reactive, to approach a level where all problems can be predicted and will be prevented.

HOW TO EVALUATE ZERO BREAKDOWN PREVENTIVE MAINTENANCE

World Class Companies will need to know how to establish a preventive maintenance program. They must begin right away by determining areas of opportunity. The Maintenance team should identify where problems have occurred in the past.

Millions of dollars are wasted yearly on inadequate predictive data analysis and application of maintenance programs. An effort should be made to find out what the data is telling you about equipment problems. It is just as wasteful to replace belts and bearings every three months, even though it is required statistically once a year, as it is not to replace them at all and wait for them to wear out.

When establishing preventive maintenance in order to achieve **World Class Status**, make certain that operators of the machinery are included. It is very easy for an operator to assist in checking fluid levels or to perform minor maintenance. A **World Class Company** provides its operators with an easy-to-follow checklist for performing routine maintenance.

There are numerous, purchased computer systems available to record and track maintenance. This is worthless if nobody takes the recorded data, analyzes it and takes corrective action. Unfortunately, many companies go merrily about collecting information that they never use to improve themselves. Companies have to learn that they can't sacrifice preventive maintenance for production. It must be given top priority. Often, however, management is not concerned enough with preventive maintenance. Instead of finding ways to prevent outbreaks of problems, they spend a majority of their time putting out the fires caused by equipment problems. Management must support the benefits of preventive maintenance and understand why it is vital to achieving **World Class Status.**

1. Is there an effective preventive maintenance program in existence?

    ____Yes ____No

    If yes, is it a computerized or manual system?

    Computerized_____   Manual_____

    If computerized, indicate system name and software supplier.

    System Name_____

    Supplier_____

2. Who is responsible for mean time between failure analysis (MTBF)?

    _____

3. Do operators have a checklist prior to shift start up to check for maintenance issues?

    ____Yes   ____No

4. Is there effective communication between production scheduling and maintenance to allow for preventive maintenance when required?

    ____Yes   ____No

5. Is machine down time documented and effective measurements in place?

    ____Yes   ____No

6. Who performs P/M on Equipment?_____

    _____

7. Is Equipment maintained only on an as needed basis?

    ____Yes   ____No

8. Are work orders utilized by the maintenance department?

    ____Yes   ____No

9. How is maintenance scheduled on equipment?_____

    _____

    _____

10. Is maintenance schedule attainment measured?
    ____Yes ____No

    If so, what is the average percentage? _____

11. How many personnel are in the maintenance function?_____#

12. Is staffing and education adequate for this function?

    ____Yes ____No

13. Is there an on-going education and training program?

    ____Yes ____No

14. Define areas of opportunity: _____

    _____

    _____

    _____

    _____

15. Is maintenance schedule adhered to or is production schedule placed first?

    _____

    _____

    _____

16. Is predictive maintenance data utilized to monitor/control the process and product quality? ____Yes ____No

17. Is Maintenance consulted on the acquisition of new equipment? ____Yes ____No

18. What measurements are used to monitor maintenance performance?

_____

_____

_____

19. Are widely visible graphic displays of maintenance relating performance/progress in use? ____Yes ____No

FACTORY OF THE FUTURE

The **World Class Assessment** lays the foundation for the factory of the future and Computer Integrated Manufacturing (CIM). Our belief is that the business philosophy we have discussed throughout this book will allow you to selectively automate key production facilities and move in the direction of total factory automation and integration. In short, the factory of the future holds to the principles of JIT/TQC.

If companies treat **World Class** as a buzz-word, they may be endangering their survival as a viable concern. **World Class Companies** will take this new direction which incorporates talents and technologies just now emerging. The factory of the future is not merely the improvement of certain aspects of the business environment. Creating islands of automation is not a good plan for achieving **World Class Status**. Companies must have an evolutionary mind-set allowing them to take small steps now. The most important rule of **World Class Company** is to pare down, to remove deadwood and to concentrate on the necessary.

1. Does the corporation have a manufacturing strategy for integrating computers and automation into the manufacturing facility?

    ____Yes ____No

2. What types of automation exist today? _____

    _____

    _____

    _____

    _____

3. Is the use of robotics existing within the company?
    ___Yes ___No

    If yes, how and where are they utilized?_____

    _____

4. Is there opportunity for a plant within the plant (cell technology)?

    ___Yes ___No   Where:_____

    _____

    _____

5. Is Group Technology Employed by the company?
    ___Yes ___No

    Where:_____

    _____

6. How many areas can be relayed out to fit the JIT Manufacturing Philosophy?

   _____

   _____

   _____

7. How many people are involved in the Factory of the Future Approach?

   _____

8. Define the areas JIT/TQC can effect in the area of Automation, Robotics, Automated Handling, etc.

   _____

   _____

   _____

   _____

   _____

CHAPTER TEN

Getting
Involved
Early

QUALITY

World Class rests on the bedrock of quality. We all know that the Japanese learned how important quality was for the future in the 1950s from Dr. Deming. Up to that time, Japanese companies had a reputation for producing low quality items. Then they realized that, in order to compete, they would need to start paying attention to quality. I like to say that the Japanese bought and read the books on quality, while their American counterparts bought them and left them on their shelves. Have you ever looked at books on your manager's desk or shelf only to find that the spines have never been cracked? Now the threat of competition is driving American companies to embrace Total Quality Control for their survival.

The Japanese spent forty years getting to the point they are at today. How much time do you have? We don't have a great deal of time.

World Class means ensuring customer satisfaction through total conformance to quality requirements.

WORLD CLASS PRINCIPLES OF QUALITY

These **World Class** rules are the operating philosophy for improving quality. This philosophy requires basic principles which will govern both short-term and long-term activities. These principles are as follows:

• *A control process, such as Statistical Process Control (SPC), by which to check, measure and report both internally and externally.*

> The determination of what is to be measured is equally as important as the method or technique used. **World Class Companies** will employ SPC at the operator level, not in the quality department.

• *A program that is driven to all levels of operation.*

> The results of a quality program should be driven to all levels of the company. The information must clearly define the goals we are trying to achieve and the measurements we use. The real issue is that when we do drive quality to the operator level, management often fails to support quality at lower levels.

• *Compliance of material requirements and specifications.*

> This means cleaning up the specifications, routings, proc-

ess sheets and drawings in our companies. Our experience has shown that you will find 50 percent of the problems uncovered by this assessment occur in the engineering phase. **World Class Status** requires 100% quality of specifications.

• *The support of management/behavior.*

Management support/behavior is the oil which keeps the machinery of quality improvement functioning smoothly. Its presence is critical to the morale and encouragement of all levels of the organization. If the different levels of the company don't feel that management is involved and committed, then their support and contributions will be limited. **World Class** demands quality behavior daily.

• *A new mind-set and culture.*

World Class fosters a culture which accepts high quality only. A zero-defect mentality must permeate all levels of a company. There must be established and clear lines of authority. Operators must be given the authority and responsibility for quality.

1. Does the company have a Quality Statement charter or vision?
    ____Yes ____No
    (Attach)

2. What percentage of manufacturing operations are under the control of Statistical Process Control (SPC)?

    <10%____ 11%-40%____ 41%-80%____ 81%-94%____ >95%____

3. What percentage of suppliers have signed quality agreements consistent with Total Quality Control (TQC)?

    <10%_____ 11%-40%____ 41%-80%____ 81%-94%____
    >95%____

4. Is there a Supplier Certification Program in Place?

    ____Yes ____No

    If yes, what percent of suppliers ship product requiring no inspection?

    <10%____ 11%-30%____ 31%-50%____ 51%-65%____
    66%-80%____ 81%-90%____ >90%____

5. Has a supplier symposium been conducted?
    ____Yes ____No

6. How many inspectors are presently employed as part of the process?

    Incoming Inspection_____
    In-Process Inspection_____
    Finished Goods Inspection_____
    Source Inspectors_____

7. Are quality engineers working with suppliers? _
    ___Yes ____No

    If yes, do they conduct the following?

    Supplier Selection Audits   ____Yes ____No
    Continuing Audits After Selection   ____Yes ____No
    Provide On-Site Training of SPC   ____Yes ____No

8. Of the total suppliers, how many supplier engineers are there?
    _____#

9. Is Quality at the operator level? ____Yes ____No

   Describe:_____

   _____

   _____

10. What is the company's present scrap percent?_____

11. What percent of products or components are reworked at present?_____

12. What is the company's first time yield percentage?_____

13. Is all quality reporting visible to management?
    ____Yes ____No

    If yes, in what form?_____

    _____

14. Is there a Material Review Board or procedure?
    ____Yes ____No

    A. If yes, who is on Board?_____

    _____

    B. Are all suppliers notified of corrected action?

    ____Yes ____No

    C. Is the procedure a closed loop?

    ____Yes ____No

15. Does a supplier survey procedure exist? ____Yes ____No
    (Attach sample)

16. Is there a quantified Supplier Rating System in place?
____Yes ____No
(Attach Sample)

17. Is there a Supplier Audit Technique in place?
____Yes ____No
(Attach Sample)

18. Is SPC being addressed with the Supplier Base?
___Yes ___No

    If yes, how is it used?_____

    _____

19. Has a Quality Awareness Program been started?
___Yes ___No

20. Whose Quality Philosophy is being followed? Deming_____

    Juran_____   Crosby_____   Other_____

21. Has Education been conducted in the Quality Area?
___Yes ___No

       Hours per employee_____

22. Is there a working knowledge of Problem Solving Techniques?
___Yes ___No

23. Is the Fishbone Technique being employed?
____Yes ____No

    If yes, where?_____

    _____

24. Can an operator stop the line? ____Yes ____No

25. Does the company plan to participate in the Malcolm Baldrige Award in the future? ____Yes ____No

26. Does a cost of quality model exist? ____Yes ____No

27. Are quality improvement teams established?
    ____Yes ____No

    If yes, how often do they meet? ____weekly ____monthly

28. Are team measurements posted for all to see?
    ____Yes ____No

    If yes, are there tangible improvements? ____Yes ____No

29. Summarize the major Quality opportunities related to JIT/TQC:

    _____

    _____

    _____

    _____

    _____

ENGINEERING

World Class Engineering requires a commitment to design, build and manufacture a quality product up front and correctly each and every time. Products of the future will require a major reduction in the time to market and will need to be designed for producibility. When reviewing a company's Engineering area, an eye should be kept on the future. Traditional engineering will result in traditional products.

It's apparent that one tackles these problems with a team approach in which Manufacturing, Engineering, Marketing, Purchasing and Suppliers sit down with each other. Early involvement of all the participants is the key. With a Design team in place, **World Class Status** is possible, because with the team comes design integration. No one person can solve the problem alone.

When we use the term Design Team, we have in mind a broad-based group which not only includes Design Engineering, but Industrial Engineering, Manufacturing Engineering, Facilities Engineering as well as Purchasing. Such a group will go beyond design considerations, however, and involve itself with tooling, quality, supplier selection and certification, learning curves, reduction of set-up times, work simplification, and value analysis. In addition, the **World Class Manufacturer** does not ignore suggestions from suppliers. Suppliers are also experts in their field. Unfortunately, it is not the norm in U.S. manufacturing to encourage this information loop.

1. Are suppliers involved in the design of new products?

    ____Yes   ____No

    If yes, explain how: _____

    _____

2. Is there a formal engineering change control system?

    ____Yes   ____No

3. How many ECO are introduced?   ____Weekly
         ____Monthly

4. How long does it take to phase in a ECO after request?

   ____Days   ____Weeks   ____Months

5. Does the engineering group control Bill of Materials?
   ____Yes   ____No

   What percent of accuracy are the BOM?   _____%

6. How are BOMs audited? _____

   _____

7. How are routings and processes updated, and what is the frequency they are updated?

   _____

   _____

   _____

8. Are routings and processes under ECO procedures?
   ____Yes   ____No

9. How are new products introduced to manufacturing?

   _____

   _____

10. Are Supplier Processes controlled and documented?

    __ Yes __ No

11. Are design reviews conducted? ____Yes   ____No

12. Are design for producibility rules established? _____

13. How long does it take to introduce a new product? _____

14. Is a program in place to reduce the number of components?

_____

15. Does a standard part number philosophy exist? _____

16. Is engineering involved in standard packaging? _____

17. What program exists to reduce cycle time?_____

18. How long is the average life cycle of a product?_____

19. Does this function understand supply base management concepts? _____

20. Who is included in design reviews?

_____

_____

21. Are part specifications included in design reviews?

_____Yes _____No

22. Are there measurements in place to show improvement in all engineering disciplines? _____Yes _____No

If yes, where? _____

_____

23. What improvements can be made for this function?

_____

_____

CHAPTER ELEVEN

Marketing and Sales

ORDER ENTRY

This is one of the most important parts of the assessment. **World Class** means that a customer order must be processed correctly and without delay. MA/COM recently conducted a customer survey as part of their **World Class** effort. The sales team evaluated the responses and planned the necessary corrective actions for improvement.

The assessment serves as a start in your effort to gain input from customers. In this area, we are once again looking for administrative involvement in **World Class** activities.

1. How many customer orders are received each month?_____

    How many line items on each order (Average)?_____

    How many ship dates on each item (Average)?_____

2. How many open customer orders are there at any one time?

    _____

3. What are typical order-to-ship lead times quoted to customers?

    PRODUCT (LINE)   LEAD TIME

    _____   _____

    _____   _____

    _____   _____

    _____   _____

4. What is the average lead time required by customers in your industry? _____

5. What percent of orders are shipped by the promised date?_____

6. Is the promised date the customer request/required date?
    ____Yes ____No

7. Does manufacturing have input in determining promise date?
    ____Yes ____No

8. What is the average number of days late of all orders?_____

9. What is the percentage (on average) of line item fill? _____%

10. How is a customer notified of late shipment?_____

11. When is a customer notified of late shipment?
    ____Problem Discovery   ____Ship Date   ____After Ship Date

12. What type of order changes are experienced between order entry and shipment?

    Additions?_____

    Deletions?_____

    Date Changes?_____

    Quantity Changes?_____

    Specification Changes?_____

    Ship to Changes?_____

    Other_____

13. Who specifies the mode of transportation/carrier?_____

14. Is there a certification program for carriers?
        ____Yes   ____No

15. What percent of sales do service part orders represent?_____

16. What customer service policies does the company have?

    _____

    _____

    _____

17. How long does it take to enter an order?
    ____Days ____Hours

18. Are shipments from stock or made to order?
    ____Stock ____Made to Order

19. Is there an application for BOM configuration type module?

    _____

    _____

20. What is the staffing level of this function?_____

    _____

21. How are customer orders promised in relationship to capacity?

    _____

    _____

FORECAST AND PLANNING

1. How do delivery dates and customer lead times get established?

   _____

   _____

   _____

2. Does management review and approve both the sales and production plan?
   ____Yes ____No

3. Does the sales forecast get recognition and reconciliation by manufacturing and sales? ____Yes ____No

   If yes, how? _____

   _____

   _____

   _____

4. How does planning get feedback from purchasing and production of any requirements that cannot be met?

   _____

   _____

   _____

5. Is the sales function informed of engineering change orders?
   ____Yes ____No

6. Is there adequate assessment of change order impact on customer delivery?

   ____Yes ____No

7. Do customer orders flow through operations and planning?

   _____

   _____

   _____

8. Describe the feedback loop for order dates or quantities that cannot be met:

_____

_____

_____

9. Are long-range manufacturing plans cognizant of market plans for new products and engineering introduction of new technologies?

____Yes ____No

How?_____

_____

_____

_____

CUSTOMER SATISFACTION

Expanding upon the base provided by excellent delivery performance, it is vital to measure the total scope of customer satisfaction in determining **World Class Status**. We must consider reputation, image and ultimately sales which are a function of product quality, price/value perception, delivery, innovation and many intangibles. While measurements in this area are sometimes imprecise, they are essential in providing a litmus test of performance in the marketplace. Measurements should include:

1. Percent of repeat sales to existing customer base _____

2. Number of complaints against orders shipped _____

3. Number of satisfaction against orders shipped _____

4. Warranty claims

    Number of occurrences by type/by customer _____

    Number of re- occurrences by type/by customer _____

    Warranty dollars $_____

    Number of repairs by age category of the product _____

5. Unquantified measurements

    Market surveys on performance (quality, delivery, function, etc.)

    Internal customer surveys (employee surveys)

6. Are other functional areas, besides customer service, used to survey/contact customers? (e.g., production workers, etc.)
    ____Yes ____No

7. Are customers included in the design review process/design for producibility?

    ____Yes ____No

8. How would you describe your reputation with the majority of your customers?

    _____

    _____

    _____

THE MARKET

How well a company can meet its customers' requirements with zero defects (ZD) is a direct function of how well they know and communicate with the marketplace.

1. What is (are) the target market(s) or segment(s)?

    _____

    _____

    _____

2. What is the size of the market? $_____

    # of potential customers _____

3. What is your market share? $_____

    # of customers _____

4. What percent of business is represented by your three largest customers?_____

5. Are they in an industry subject to dramatic business cycles? (e.g., nuclear, oil and gas, defense, etc.) _____Yes _____No

6. Is there a formal marketing plan? _____Yes _____No

7. Is there a marketing forecast:

    In dollars? _____Yes _____No
    By product line? _____Yes _____No
    By SKU(s)? _____Yes _____No

8. Who are your competitors?

_____

_____

_____

9. What are their estimated market shares?

   <u>Company</u>   <u>%</u>

   _____   _____

   _____   _____

   _____   _____

   _____   _____

10. What is your pricing structure/strategy?

   "Skim the cream" _____
   "Middle of the road" _____
   Commodity _____
   "Cheap style" _____

11. What is your strategy with respect to price changes?

   "Market leader" _____
   "Me too" _____
   "Hold the line" _____
   Other (specify) _____

12. Do you have a minimum, planned acceptable margin?
   ____Yes ____No

If by product line, specify: <u>Product</u>   <u>Percent</u>

_____   _____

_____   _____

_____   _____

_____   _____

13. Where is your technological and product image/position in the marketplace?

Innovator/High tech _____

Commodity _____

Other (specify) _____

14. Is there a short-term growth strategy? ____Yes ____No

15. What is it? _____

_____

_____

_____

16. Is there a long-term growth strategy? ____Yes ____No

17. What is it? _____

_____

_____

_____

18. What new product(s) are under development/introduction?

_____

_____

_____

19. Are you planning to enter any new markets?
    ____Yes ____No

    When? _____

20. Are they "me too" or market leaders? _____

21. Is the competition developing/introducing any new or response product(s)?

    ____Yes ____No

22. What are they? _____

_____

_____

_____

23. Are any of your competitors' patented products or processes about to expire? ____Yes ____No

24. What products/processes? _____

_____

_____

_____

25. When? ____Day ____Month ____Year

26. Who are your competitors' major/critical suppliers?

_____

_____

_____

27. Are they also yours? ____Yes ____No

   If yes, who? _____

_____

_____

_____

28. Does your marketing group actively and regularly participate in **World Class** (JIT/TQC) education and training?

   ____Yes ____No

29. Do you have performance measurements to monitor your marketing strategy/plan?

   ____Yes ____No

   What are they? _____

_____

_____

_____

SALES

The sales force represents your company to the customer. It is essential that they believe in and practice the **World Class** mind-set, in their day-to-day dealings with the customer base.

1. Do you sell direct or through distributors?

   ____Direct ____Distributors ____Both

2. Do you employ your own sales force, manufacturers reps or both?

   ___Own ____Mfr. reps ____Both

3. Does your company have a formal sales plan?
   ____Yes ____No

4. What growth percentage is planned?

   ____1st year ____2nd year ____3rd year

5. Is the market national or regional? _____

6. How many sales personnel do you employ? (own force and/or manfacturers reps) _____

7. Do they set specific prices by customer/market segments?
   ____Yes ____No

8. Do they "validate" promised delivery dates with manufacturing?
   ____Yes ____No

9. Do they provide written feedback on quality, delivery, price-value, performance, etc. from the customer base?
   ____Yes ____No

10. Does your sales force actively and regularly participate in **World Class** (JIT/TQC) education and training?
    ____Yes ____No

11. Do you have performance measurements to monitor the sales plan and/or personnel?
    ____Yes ____No

    What are they? _____

    _____

    _____

    _____

ADVERTISING AND PROMOTION

The image of a company is to a great extent dependent on its ability to communicate **World Class Status** to its current and potential customers.

1. What is your advertising and promotional budget?
   $_____

2. What is the theme or thrust of your general campaign/image development?

    _____

    _____

    _____

3. Is it regional or national? or both? _____

Do they differ? How? _____

_____

_____

_____

4. What media do you use to carry your message?
   ____Newspapers ____Radio ____TV ____Trade Journals

   ____Other (Specify) _____

5. Do you have performance measurements related to your program?

   ____Yes ____No

   What are they? _____

   _____

   _____

   _____

CHAPTER TWELVE

Overview

The objective and goal is for each company to embrace the continuous improvement mindset with a commitment, dedication and culture which is conducive to change. These qualities will significantly simplify the attainment of **World Class Status**. The most important task is to gain the support of people. More programs fail because they fall back on traditional methods, rather than providing employees with responsibility and authority during the implementation process.

In reviewing the approach of many companies, we often find a lack of leadership, planning and direction. Many companies feel that when they educate the workers the responsibility for the program's success has passed from management to direct labor. These same companies, however, fail to realize the human issues involved and how to create an environment for the **World Class** process.

Attaining **World Class Status** requires support, not criticism, and the total endorsement of the program by management within the company. In order to do this, data gathering must be developed early in the program. The suggestions in this section are intended to provide you with a global picture of the company and its requirements.

1. Review each of the following areas and identify the potential for improvement:

	PRESENT	POTENTIAL
Customer delivery performance	_____	_____
Manufacturing lead time (Reduction)	_____	_____
Quality Improvement (Cost of Quality)	_____	_____
Set Up Time (Reduction)	_____	_____
Layout of Manufacturing (cells. group technology)	_____	_____
New Product Introduction	_____	_____
Working Environment	_____	_____
Inventory Levels	_____	_____
Obsolete Inventory	_____	_____
Excess Inventory	_____	_____
Inventory Turns	_____	_____
Idle Time/Overtime	_____	_____
Lead Time	_____	_____

2. Set-up time measured in: Seconds_____ Minutes_____
Hours_____ Shifts_____ Days_____

Is there a potential opportunity for significant improvements?
_____Yes _____No

If yes, where are the areas of immediate payback? Define
both short term and long term objectives:

_____

_____

3. Identify the potential improvements in the following areas: (%
improvement)

Reduced Idle Time_____

More Effective use of Equipment_____

Expediting_____

Manufacturing Cost_____

Total Cost_____

Scrap Reduction_____

Rework Reduction_____

Salvage Reduction_____

Obsolescence_____

Reduced Rework_____

Reduced Line Stoppage_____

Capital Expenditures_____

Tooling Expenditures_____

Preventive Maintenance_____

Equipment up-time_____

4. If the JIT philosophy was fully employed, indicate the effects it will have on the operation.

    Work-In-Process_____

    Finished Goods Inventory_____

    Raw Material_____

    Customer Service_____

    Sales Revenue_____

    Shortages_____

    Employee Involvement_____

    Reduced Overtime_____

5. Determine the current amount of support from each functional area to JIT/TQC:

	HEAVY	MODERATE	NON EXISTENT
Top Management	_____	_____	_____
Engineering	_____	_____	_____
Purchasing	_____	_____	_____
Finance	_____	_____	_____
Plant Management	_____	_____	_____
Production Scheduling	_____	_____	_____
Inventory Control	_____	_____	_____
Data Processing	_____	_____	_____

	HEAVY	MODERATE	NON EXISTENT
Quality	_____	_____	_____
Traffic	_____	_____	_____
Cost Accounting	_____	_____	_____
Sales	_____	_____	_____
Marketing	_____	_____	_____
Order Entry	_____	_____	_____
Direct labor	_____	_____	_____

COST/BENEFIT ANALYSIS

World Class Manufacturers will need to educate their employees about value-added and cost/benefit analyses. We make it easy by initiating the following questions:

COST

- **What's it going to cost in materials, machine time and labor to make the improvement?**

BENEFIT

- **What's it going to benefit you in labor, materials, productivity and machine time once the improvement is made?**

After we walk them through how to answer these questions, teams find it easy to calculate a cost/benefit analysis. It is gratifying to watch a team learn the process of cost justification. Teams made up of the real experts from the floor are more than capable of sophisticated analyses when given the proper training. We have never failed to see a well educated and trained team learn how to problem-solve or perform a cost/benefit analysis.

Calculate the following benefits analyses for the attached schedules A-E:

SCHEDULE A
POTENTIAL BENEFITS ANALYSIS
INVENTORY REDUCTION MODEL

WHAT IS THE COST OF GOODS SOLD? $_____   DIVIDED BY:

WHAT IS THE ON HAND INVENTORY? $_____   =_____
                                INVENTORY TURNS

ON HAND INVENTORY $_____X .1025= $_____
                                INVENTORY COST

ON HAND INVENTORY $_____X ____= $_____
                   Carrying Cost C.C.%   INVENTORY COST

75% REDUCTION MODEL

    INVENTORY COST $_____X   .75= $_____
                                SAVINGS

50% REDUCTION MODEL

    INVENTORY COST $_____X   .50= $_____
                                SAVINGS

25% REDUCTION MODEL

    INVENTORY COST $_____X   .25= $_____
                                SAVINGS

                    SAVINGS $_____

SCHEDULE B
POTENTIAL BENEFITS ANALYSIS
SET UP REDUCTION MODEL

CURRENT SET UP TIME IN HOURS PER WEEK _____

CURRENT AVERAGE HOURLY WAGE FOR THOSE PERFORMING SET UPS $_____

_____ X $_____ = $_____ X 52= $_____
HOURS/WEEK   WAGES/HOUR   ANNUAL SET-UP
                                            COSTS

75% REDUCTION MODEL

$_____ X .75 = $_____
ANNUAL SET   SAVINGS
UP COSTS

50% REDUCTION MODEL

$_____ X .50 = $_____
ANNUAL SET   SAVINGS
UP COSTS

25% REDUCTION MODEL

$_____ X .25 = $_____
ANNUAL SET   SAVINGS
UP COSTS

                                 SAVINGS $_____

SCHEDULE C
POTENTIAL BENEFITS ANALYSIS
PRODUCTIVITY IMPROVEMENT MODEL

CURRENT NUMBER OF DIRECT EMPLOYEES _____ TIMES
AVERAGE WAGE PER HOUR OF DIRECT EMPLOYEES $_____
X 1900 * = TOTAL WAGES $_____

30% REDUCTION OF DIRECT LABOR COSTS

$_____ X .30 = $_____
TOTAL WAGES   SAVINGS

20% REDUCTION OF DIRECT LABOR COSTS

$_____ X .20 = $_____
TOTAL WAGES   SAVINGS

10% REDUCTION OF DIRECT LABOR COSTS

$_____ X .10 = $_____
TOTAL WAGES   SAVINGS

SAVINGS $_____

* Note: 250 days x 7.6 hr per day.

SCHEDULE D
POTENTIAL BENEFITS ANALYSIS
COST OF QUALITY IMPROVEMENT MODEL

CURRENT COST OF QUALITY(COQ)

FAILURE	$_____
APPRAISAL	$_____
PREVENTIVE	$_____
TOTAL	$_____

60% REDUCTION MODEL

$$\underset{\text{TOTAL COQ}}{\$_____} \text{ X } .60 = \underset{\text{SAVINGS}}{\$_____}$$

40% REDUCTION MODEL

$$\underset{\text{TOTAL COQ}}{\$_____} \text{ X } .40 = \underset{\text{SAVINGS}}{\$_____}$$

20% REDUCTION MODEL

$$\underset{\text{TOTAL COQ}}{\$_____} \text{ X } .20 = \underset{\text{SAVINGS}}{\$_____}$$

SAVINGS $_____

The previous schedules are guidelines which you should use to address the major topics of waste reduction. Each company will find its own areas of improvement. The intangible savings noted below can be determined by reviewing the entire assessment. Your most important job is to establish a base line and mark your improvement from that point.

<u>SCHEDULE E</u>
<u>POTENTIAL BENEFITS ANALYSIS</u>
<u>SUMMARY</u>

INVENTORY SAVINGS (SCHEDULE A) $_____

SET UP SAVINGS (SCHEDULE B) $_____

PRODUCTIVITY IMPROVEMENT SAVINGS
                    (SCHEDULE C) $_____

COST OF QUALITY SAVINGS
                    (SCHEDULE D) $_____

INTANGIBLE SAVINGS $_____

TOTAL PROJECTED SAVINGS $_____

Describe the tangible and intangible effect the following list will have on Potential Benefits and Savings:

CUSTOMER SATISFACTION_____

_____

SPACE AVAILABILITY DUE TO LESS INVENTORY_____

_____

YOUR COMPANY BECOMES COMPETITIVE IN THE
WORLD   MARKET_____

_____

EMPLOYEE INVOLVEMENT (SATISFACTION OF WORKER)

_____

_____

INCREASED FLEXIBILITY_____

_____

MANAGEMENT BURDEN REDUCED _____

_____

DISCIPLINED MANUFACTURING PROCESS

_____

_____

QUICK PRODUCT INTRODUCTION_____

_____

INCREASED SAFETY_____

_____

SALARIED STAFF PRODUCTIVITY IMPROVEMENT_____

_____

REDUCED INSPECTION_____

_____

SUPPLIER RELATIONS IMPROVED_____

_____

SUPPLIER QUALITY IMPROVED_____

_____

REDUCTION OF INCOMING INSPECTION_____

_____

REDUCED TRANSPORTATION COST_____

_____

DESIGN FOR PRODUCIBILITY_____

_____

CHAPTER THIRTEEN

How to Utilize the World Class Assessment

There are numerous scales that can be developed to evaluate responses to the **World Class Assessment**. We have included some examples of the more useful ones in this chapter. Self-evaluation, of course, requires a considerable amount of objectivity which a consultant can provide through independent findings. Chances are excellent that a team will bring the required amount of objectivity to the task if they are properly directed. A team should rate the company based on the answers given in appropriate sections of the **World Class Assessment**. Indeed, how honest you are in evaluating your company will be an indication of your ability to attain **World Class**. This assessment is needed to establish, with brutal honesty, where a company stands against its competition throughout the world. As we have said before, not knowing where you stand now may result in your not standing at all in the future.

TOP MANAGEMENT COMMITMENT

A necessary element of **World Class Status** is top management's commitment to the change process and the creation of a company culture which fosters responsibility, authority, vision and accountability at the lowest level. One of the most important indicators of management commitment is their behavior as the rest of the company tests the process.

Management must continue to ask "What are we doing and how are we doing?" and accept answers which may be difficult to hear. Management commitment means creating an environment where creative problem-solving behavior is the norm. The **World Class Assessment** prepares the company to evaluate potential opportunities and prepare a realistic plan. People are very suspicious of plans with vision statements which make them wary of yet another program handed down from on high. A recent article in the *Wall Street Journal* pointed out that DuPont is having problems with its quality circles. I remember telling a management group last year that a program of this nature will not work without "buy in" from union personnel. When a vision statement ends up as a management program, the results you obtain are less than desired.

Below are the major commitments for which people in a **World Class** environment are looking:

TOP MANAGEMENT REQUIREMENTS

	YES	NO
• Establish goals and objectives which can be reached.	____	____
• Use patience and persistence in working with people. (Listen) (Silent)	____	____

YES NO

- Develop a trust with your people, suppliers and customers. (Partnership)   ____ ____

- Improve communications with suppliers and customers. (Partnership)   ____ ____

- Delegate responsibility, authority, vision and accountability to the *operator level*. (Operator can stop the line.)   ____ ____

- Adopt a no-waste attitude. (Zero defects)   ____ ____

- Allocate/authorize financial support and measurements. (Total Cost)   ____ ____

- Devote resources to project teams. (Employee involvement and capital)   ____ ____

- Risk short-term operational results for long-term improvements. (Total Cost)   ____ ____

- Foster interdepartmental communication and cooperation. (Team Building)   ____ ____

- Follow up, monitor, document and measure. (Performance measurements)   ____ ____

- Establish an on-going training and education program. (Continuous Improvement Process)   ____ ____

- Listen to the experts—your people. (Different Set of Eyes)   ____ ____

- Correct processes, rather than rework parts. (Statistical Process Control)   ____ ____

- Foster a "no waiver" environment and attitude in processes and specifications. (Fitness for Use)   ____ ____

- Develop a reward mechanism for achievements. (Employee Involvement)   ____ ____

There are 16 criteria in the above list. Place a check in the "Yes" column, if your company has a program to accomplish what is stated. Place a check in the "No" column, if no program exists. Add up all the "Yes" and "No" answers. Use the grid below to calculate your status.

Level	Description	No. of Positive Responses	Results
1	Little or no comprehension of World Class Status	0 -4	Go out of business
2	Recognize value, but no management commitment	5-8	Profit erosion
3	Willing to learn and support the process	9-12	Change in process
4	Participating in World Class Program	13-15	Culture changed
5	Program is integrated part of company thinking	16	World Class Status

Crucial indicators of a company's potential to be **World Class** are company-wide in nature. At Level One, a company's management has little or no comprehension of **World Class** practices and philosophies such as Just-In-Time or Total Quality Control. Tasks are performed in the same ways as they were twenty years ago. Level Two management is aware of what must be done, but have not committed the necessary dollars and resources to the program. Management rises to the Level Three when they are willing to learn and support **World Class** programs and initiate a process of people involvement. At Level Four, management is actively participating in all levels of **World Class** program requirements. Level Five is the goal that we strive to attain—**World Class Status**. At this level, management sees both the status of the company as a whole and the status of its customers and suppliers as an integral part of the company.

EMPLOYEE INVOLVEMENT

In a very real sense, achieving **World Class Status** is not a program for management alone. There is little chance of success if a company does not involve workers on the plant floor. **World Class Excellence** demands that you recognize the importance of all people, that you provide them with the responsibility and authority to act on their own to further the company's objectives. If you fail to treat them with high regard, your primary source of new and creative ideas and solutions to problems will dry up like a lake in a desert. Fortunately, being creative is one of the most enjoyable activities at any person's job. Thus, getting employees involved in a **World Class** program requires no more from management than allowing people the time and means to express their natural abilities, to be creative, to find solutions, to work as a team in a non-threatening environment. We must overcome those past feelings of mistrust which have kept people from expressing their natural creativity if we are to survive in the future.

The following list would characterize a company who has achieved **World Class Status** in the area of employee involvement:

- A fair and equitable reward and incentive system is in place.

- The employee suggestion program is clearly defined and used.

- Labor (union and non-union) fears and issues are addressed in an open and honest atmosphere.

- Information is freely shared. There are no hidden agendas or agencies.

- The issue of job classifications and job security have been clearly faced and resolved.

- Management and supervisory levels have been reduced to reporting levels.

- There is a continuous training and education program present throughout the company.

How many of these characteristics show up on your **World Class Assessment**?

GUIDELINES FOR PURCHASING'S NEW ROLE

A second Industrial Revolution has reduced costs associated with labor and operations to the point where they account for less than 20% of product costs while material acquisition costs comprise over 60%.

Quite obviously, Purchasing and the Material Management have an opportunity to contribute directly to a company's achievement of **World Class Status**. Purchasing has a new role in an age where a Total Business Concept is fast becoming the norm, and, even more importantly, a necessity for survival. The six guidelines below will help you establish the goals, scope, objectives and foundation of this new role.

GUIDELINES FOR PURCHASING'S NEW ROLE

1. **DEVELOPMENT OF SUPPLIER BASE MANAGE-MENT** — Purchasing must develop a partnership with suppliers which is based on trust. Purchasing must be aware of production schedules, supplier problems, financial considerations, sales forecasts, marketing research and customer needs—in short, company-wide goals—which are communicated to suppliers.

2. **SUPPLIER SELECTION CRITERIA** — The challenge is to select qualified suppliers early in the process. The objective is a certification program which will create a foundation for the future. A supplier who possesses all the right capabilities is more likely to become an excellent partner who will help in controlling total cost.

3. **LONG-TERM RELATIONSHIPS WITH SUPPLIERS** — Purchasing must develop suppliers for the life of a product or for a long term. In this environment, both sides can work together as partners in their attempts to reduce costs and improve quality.

4. **SUPPLIER CERTIFICATION** — This guideline is the foundation of supplier development, tone of the tenets of

the Total Business Concept (TBC). Purchasing must establish a zero-defect program with suppliers in order to remain competitive.

5. **SUPPLIER SURVEY AND AUDIT** — Purchasing must use surveys and audits to insure that suppliers have a quality control system in place which subscribes to the same zero-defect goals and process controls as your company does. We can't afford to waste time and money on suppliers who accept poor quality or who don't want to enter into a partnership.

6. **ELECTRONIC DATA INTERCHANGE (EDI)** — EDI will help you achieve "paperless purchasing" as well as create an indispensable pool of common data. It is a long-term objective to eliminate waste in Purchasing.

SUPPLIER RATING SYSTEM

A **World Class Manufacturer** is a company whose suppliers have been certified in a Supplier Certification program. Another criterion is suppliers who are capable of entering into long-term agreements for 3-5 years or the life of a product. In these agreements, it is stipulated that both you and the supplier will work together on:

> **Product Cost Reduction**
> **Quality Attainment and Product Specifications**
> **Value Engineering**
> **Total Cost Reduction**

The supplier selection team's next task is to determine what are the basic requirements to become a certified supplier and the key questions to ask when selecting a supplier. A Supplier Rating system should include at least the following parts:

1   Management commitment to quality:
— Published quality statement.
— Training.
— Quality councils.
— Process improvement plans.

2   Established quality process in place.

3   Quality measurements in use:
— Cost of quality.
— Control charts/statistics.
— Number of defects.

4   Improvement philosophy demonstrated.

5   Future quality goals in place.

6   Quality improvement process implemented.

7   Quality evidence available for product.

8   Demonstrated performance.

9   Prevention-oriented quality process in use.

WORLD CLASS STATUS

World Class Status is achieved by a number of different routes which makes it difficult to develop one matrix to cover all business environments. Contrary to what many experts say, **World Class** is not achieved simply by converting only one factory cell or one JIT line to the principles outlined in this book. **World Class** means that the whole company subscribes to and practices these principles. That is not easily achieved, but when it is, it means a great deal. The questions and matrix below provide a nucleus for you to use in evaluating your company's status and for planning your strategy to achieve **World Class Status**. Note that what we have provided is the minimum which is required.

Answer the questions below with a "yes" or "no":

YES	NO	
____	____	Organizational structure defines quality responsibility and authority at the lowest level.
____	____	Top management is accessible daily to direct labor.
____	____	An education and training program exists (minimum of two hours per employee).
____	____	Formal deviation and corrective action procedure results in specifications being changed to conform with actual.
____	____	Certified suppliers are used instead of inspection techniques.

YES   NO

____   ____   Procedures for storage, release and movement of material have high degree of accuracy and lot traceability.

____   ____   Work-in-process material is at a minimum.

____   ____   Process capabilities are established and controlled by operators.

____   ____   Procedures for equipment and facility preventive maintenance programs are present.

____   ____   Statistical Process Control is employed at operator level.

____   ____   Management has an effective and comprehensive long-term, **World Class** business plan.

____   ____   A continuous training and education program exists for all employees.

____   ____   Safety and housekeeping audits are scheduled on a regular basis. (Good Manufacturing Practices)

____   ____   Process control information is used to identify the root causes of problems.

YES   NO

_____   _____   Personnel are trained in problem-solving techniques.

_____   _____   Delivery time is measured (e.g., the percentage of deliveries made on time).

_____   _____   A Set-Up Reduction program exists.

How many of the questions did you answer with a "yes"? The matrix below will show you how close your company is to attaining **World Class Status** in this area.

No. of "Yes" Responses	Rating
0 - 5	**Little or no comprehension of World Class Status.**
6 - 8	**Recognize value, but no commitment of dollars.**
9 - 12	**Willing to learn and support.**
13 - 15	**Participating in World Class Program.**
16 - 17	**World Class Status.**

In the next chapter, we will look at how your company can raise your score. We will discuss a method of implementation which has proven successful in a variety of different manufacturing environments, industries and countries.

CHAPTER FOURTEEN

Implementing the World Class Process

Once the **World Class Assessment** is completed and reviewed, the next step is to begin an implementation process which will result in the achievement of **World Class Status**. The key to this implementation process is to involve the whole company.

The first stage in the implementation process is **training and education**. This is followed by the establishment of a **steering committee** and then the establishment of **teams** which will attack and solve problems. Lastly, measurements must be put in place in order to compare today's status with established benchmarks and objectives.

COMPETENCY MODEL

Training and education is a tool to help your business meet its objectives today and in the future. A company has the responsibility of ensuring that its staff is properly evaluated and then trained. The goal, then, is to provide a positive atmosphere which will stimulate employees to discuss theory, practices and alternatives. Training should be based on job competency and focused on

Competency Model for Determining Knowledge and Skill Requirements By Function

COMPETENCY AREAS	FUNCTIONS							
	Marketing	Finance	Sales	Production	Quality	Purchasing	Planning	Traffic
JIT Principles	3	3	3	3	3	3	3	3
Set-up Reduction	1	2	1	3	3	3	3	1
Supplier Certification	2	1	2	3	3	3	3	3
SPC/TQC	1	1	1	3	3	3	3	2
Preventive Maint.	1	1	1	3	1	1	2	1
Value Analysis	1	1	1	3	3	3	3	2
Problem-solving	3	3	3	3	3	3	3	3
MRP II	2	3	2	3	2	3	3	3

1. indicates a familiarity with subject
2. requires a working knowledge of field
3. requires expertise in area

creating greater cross-functional awareness. Training and education must become a way of life in your company. It's a way of life whose end result is to give workers the tools for continuous improvement.

The first priority in planning a training and education program in **World Class** is to assess needs and opportunities. We have developed a competency model which will assist you in defining where your company is proficient or deficient. The numbers indicate the necessary levels of expertise for each function. By comparing the levels of expertise within your company to the desired levels in the chart, you can determine short-term and long-term objectives in your education and training program.

EDUCATION AND TRAINING

We recommend that every employee be provided an opportunity to receive some education in **World Class** topics. Education encourages cross-fertilization of ideas and develops generalists, instead of specialists. Education must provide the following:

- **A clear understanding of World Class Objectives.**
- **A positive climate to express ideas without fear.**
- **An environment for active participation.**
- **Time to solve problems.**
- **System to measure success.**

Education is learning the theory behind what you are doing; training is putting into practice what you have learned. Education must occur at all levels of a company. Contrary to traditional educational methods used by many companies where more time is spent teaching direct labor than management, we invert the educational pyramid as shown below:

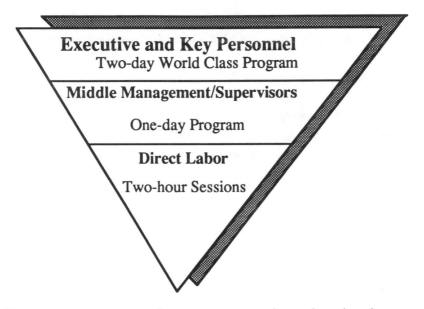

Top management receives more extensive education because without their understanding and commitment, the rest of your education and training program will go nowhere. It is an undeniable fact that workers look to their leaders for direction. A middle manager or direct laborer is more apt to embrace **World Class** if he or she sees a vice president committed to the program.

THE STEERING COMMITTEE

A company must establish a steering committee to manage the implementation of **World Class**. The steering committee should consist of no more than 10 people from all levels of the company, from top management to direct labor, with an equal balance of each. The role of the steering committee is to **organize** the company's program around clearly stated aims and goals.

Another task of the steering committee is to **staff** teams with volunteers. The general rule is that a team should have eight to ten members and that for every salaried or management person, there should be an hourly laborer. When a team gets above twelve people, there is a tendency for the team to get bogged down. It is a good idea at this point to form sub-teams or to divide the existing team into two groups. Teams should also represent a cross-section of the company.

The steering committee also has the responsibility of **directing** teams. This means that once every four to six weeks the individual team leaders must present a ten-minute overview to the committee. In this report, the team leader must tell what the team has accomplished in the last period. The steering committee must quickly resolve any issues which arise.

TEAM MANAGEMENT

One characteristic of the Far East which helps them achieve **World Class Status** is their sense of teamwork. Companies must emphasize and reward teamwork. Some people confuse teams with consensus management or a slowly moving company that can't make a decision. The teams we advocate are quite the opposite. We define a team as the following:

TEAM (*n*)—A group of people dedicated to a common goal who have learned to build on each other's strengths and to compensate for each others' weaknesses.

We have to get rid of the "hand grenade" mentality in which one person or department thinks it's doing well and that everybody else is doing poorly. We want to break down these barriers to improvement.

PROBLEM-SOLVING TECHNIQUES

Problem-solving techniques are widely misused and underutilized. When was the last time you saw a senior management group making a Pareto list of causes and then drawing a cause enumeration fishbone? Not often, I'm sure. The tendency of many companies is to use the first solution which pops up. This is not a problem-solving technique; it's a band-aid solution. We need problem-solving like what is discussed next to show up at even the top levels of a company.

The form on the next page should be used in problem-solving. The key element here is that what we formerly labeled a problem was in reality a symptom. Symptoms consist of many causes, each of which is an opportunity to be solved by the team.

The team uses this form by listing all of the possible reasons why a particular symptom could be occurring. The third column points out the vital few, or root causes of the problem. The team's mission is to find the two or three causes which would make the majority of the symptoms disappear.

The next step is to find *ways to eliminate* each of these root causes. The key words here are "ways" and "eliminate." We need to look beyond the first solution which comes to mind and we must be sure that each solution positively "kills" the problem.

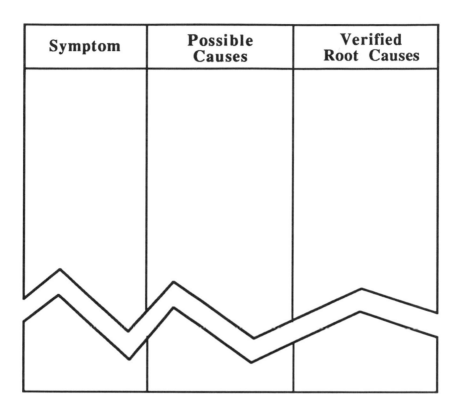

Symptom	Possible Causes	Verified Root Causes

In the next chapter, we will look at how a **World Class Company** can measure its success at continuous improvement. We will explore measurements which your company will find useful.

CHAPTER FIFTEEN

World Class Measurements

The **World Class Company's** hardest task is to establish meaningful measurements. Take a look at the various measurements gathered while you were completing the **World Class Assessment**. How many of your current measurements complement and interface with each other? For example, does Purchasing measure Purchase Price Variance (PPV) while the factory measures Machine Utilization or Production Schedule Attainment? While Purchasing drives prices down, the cost of manufacturing rockets upward. This is one example of many measurement conflicts in a company.

We must be sure that all measurements are interrelated for the achievement of **World Class Status**. The key is to establish a benchmark today with goals and objectives which must be accomplished. Once a base is established, companies measure and monitor their progress toward the goal. Perhaps most importantly measurements are useful as a dynamic management tool which establishes a results orientation in the workplace. Measurement graphs like the ones below should be displayed throughout the plant for people to see.

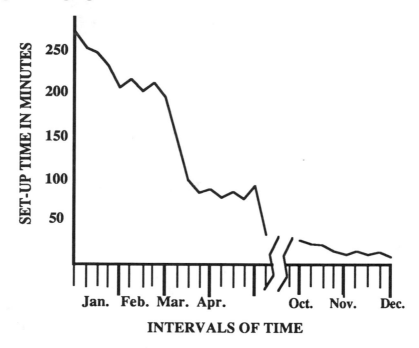

SET-UP REDUCTION
MEASUREMENT GRAPH

Formulas:

Number of Hours Involved ÷ Total Hours = %

Nuber of Hours per Week in Set-up x Standard Hourly Rate

Number of Set-up Hours Reduced by Dept. x Standard Hourly Rate

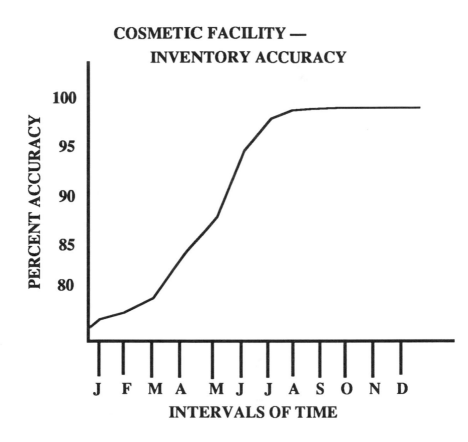

**COSMETIC FACILITY —
INVENTORY ACCURACY**

Accuracy is a measurement of the number of accurate/correct items (both in quality and location) against the number selected for counting.

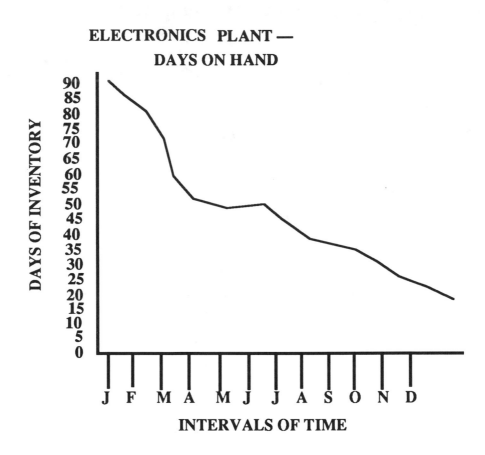

ELECTRONICS PLANT —
DAYS ON HAND

This measurement tracks actual performance of the plant's inventory segments and total against budgeted/forecast for inventory investment by day, week and month.

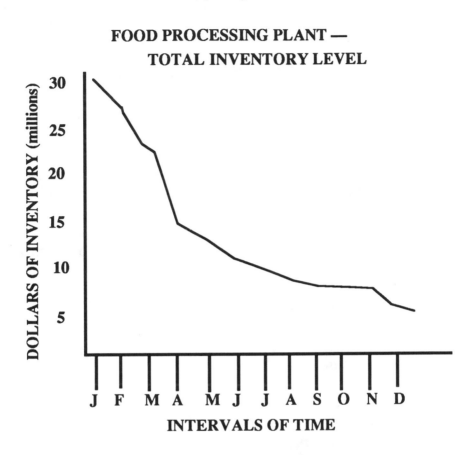

**FOOD PROCESSING PLANT —
TOTAL INVENTORY LEVEL**

Actual example of a twelve-month World Class Program. This company freed up 39% of their space containing inventory.

ENGINEERING MEASUREMENTS

Time To Design

Purpose: This measurement tracks the scedule versus actual time taken to generate a product design. A design should include any and all appropriate documentation called for to release the product to manufacturing. Drawings, bills of material, routings and any other internal or external paperwork or instruction should be included in the design time.

Responsibility: Engineering should be responsible for quoting the time for design, and also for measuring the actual time taken.

Reporting: Reports or graphs should be established per product, project or part being designed. If the activity involves a change that is being redesigned, then separate categories should be maintained.

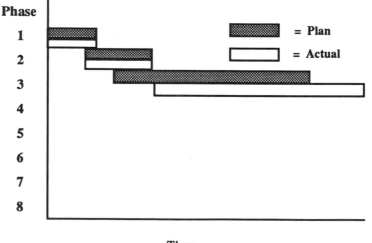

Time to Design — Phases of Development

Cost for Design allows the project person to see how well the project is doing and provides Manufacturing with an idea of what might be coming. You should analyze issues which cause a project to fall behind schedule and take action and prevent recurrence.

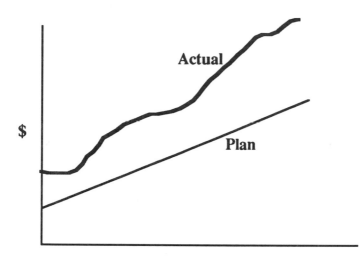

Time
Cost to Design

Measuring the Number of ECO's (Engineering Change Orders)

Purpose: This measurement allows a company to track the number of changes to drawings, documentation, specifications and products. Use this measurement to analyze the causes of changes.

Responsibility: Engineering should be held responsible for the number of changes. ECO's are considered waste and reflect not being able to do the job right the first time.

Reporting: Each type of ECO should be tracked and graphed in order to allow the company to capture data related to the cost of each change. The number of open ECOs should be displayed on a graph. The goal is to reduce the number over time.

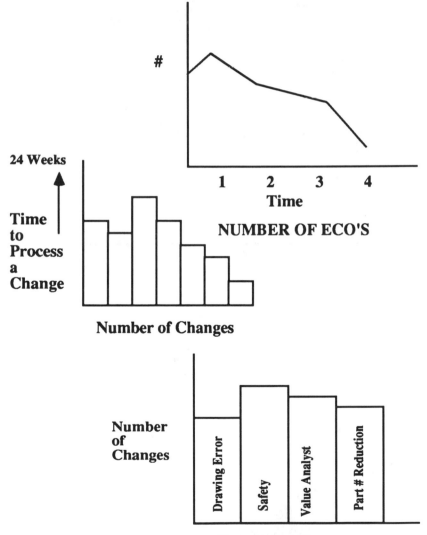

Cost of Engineering Change Orders

Cost = Labor + production lost + material lost.

Labor lost = Engineering + manufacturing + materials (people) + processing + testing + inspection.

Production lost = Product built (scrapped or disassembled) + rework + lost sales.

Materials lost = Obsolete inventory + purchase order + cancellations.

Other engineering performance measurements to consider:

- Number of waivers by time period to validate specification correctness.
- Number of engineering changes requested.
- Number of engineering changes processed.
- Aged number of changes requested and processed.

PURCHASING MEASUREMENTS

Quantity Variances

Purpose: This measurement places an emphasis on getting the exact quantity of parts requested from suppliers. Variances, plus or minus, are used to analyze their effect on the organization.

Responsibility: Purchasing should maintain this measurement from data provided by Receiving and Inspection.

Reporting: Reports should reflect either the number short or over and the effects should be captured on a Pareto chart. Both consolidated for the supply base and separate reports should be produced for each supplier and used to capture supplier performance.

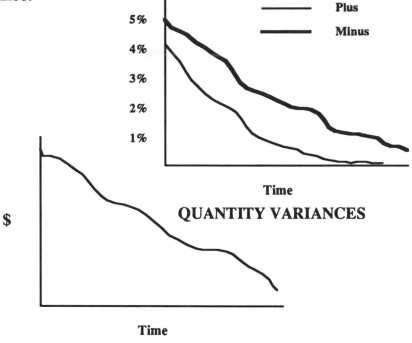

QUANTITY VARIANCES

**QUANTITY VARIANCES
IN DOLLARS**

Number of Defects

Purpose: This measurement tracks items which are received with defects from suppliers. You should analyze why and what the effect of this measurement is on your company.

Responsiblity: The responsibility for this measurement should be with Purchasing. However, the data needs to be provided by Incoming Inspection.

Reporting: The measurements should include graphs which reflect the number, percent and cost of defects. Reports should reflect performance by supplier and the total supply base.

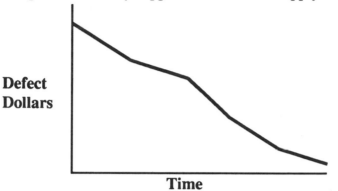

Calculation of Dollars:

Dollars = Inspection cost + processing cost + distribution cost.
Inspection cost = Cost of labor to inspect all parts to find bad ones + equipment cost + carrying cost.
Processing cost = Cost of maintaining data and records on defects.
Distribution cost = Labor to move it + packing + shipping.

On-Time Delivery

Purpose: Purchasing should track the supplier's ability to deliver to the agreed-upon date. This measurement should be communicated back to the supplier and used by Purchasing for supplier ratings.

Responsibility: In most companies , the computer system should provide Purchasing with an on-time delivery measurement. If not, the data should be collected manually by Purchasing and Receiving functions.

Reporting: This measurement should be made into a graph which reflects the variances to the delivery date. The causes should be analyzed so that internal and external improvements can be made.

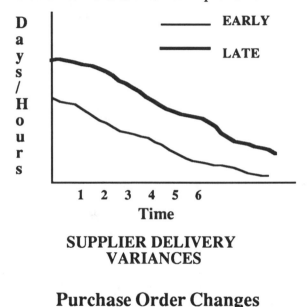

**SUPPLIER DELIVERY
VARIANCES**

Purchase Order Changes

Purpose: Allows the company to track the number of changes to Purchase Orders and analyze the reasons for the changes. The cost to make changes needs to be calculated in order to emphasize the need to improve.

Responsibility: Responsibility for this measurement should be with the purchasing department. However, the company needs to track the causes of the changes back to the function making the requisition and subsequent changes for analysis and eventual elimination of the problem.

Reporting: This measurement should be displayed in graphs which reflect the number of changes and the costs.

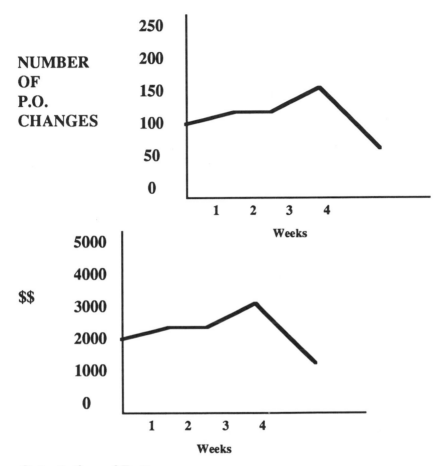

Calculation of Dollar

Dollars per week = Processing cost x number of changes.
   $7,500   =   75   x   100.
Processing cost = Time to process x rate.
      $75   =   3 hours   x $25.

Time to process = Analysis + preparing P.O. + receiving + inspection + updating records.

Rate = Average dollar of functions impacted.

Receipts to Inventory/WIP

Purpose: This measurement represents the company's efforts in moving toward the delivery of materials directly to work-in-process instead of inventory. This measurement should promote the analysis of why materials are not allowed to be delivered directly to the floor.

Responsibility: Teams should be responsible for maintaining the measurement and the activities toward continuous improvements.

Reporting: A measurement graph should reflect the percent relationship between materials going into inventory versus directly to their destinations. The cost of the intermediate stops before getting to the floor should also be calculated and reported.

Calculation of dollars:

Dollars = Labor (Price x carrying cost % x days).
$30,000 = 20.00 (20,000 x 25% x 3).

Labor = Average labor dollars to receive + count + inspect + stock.

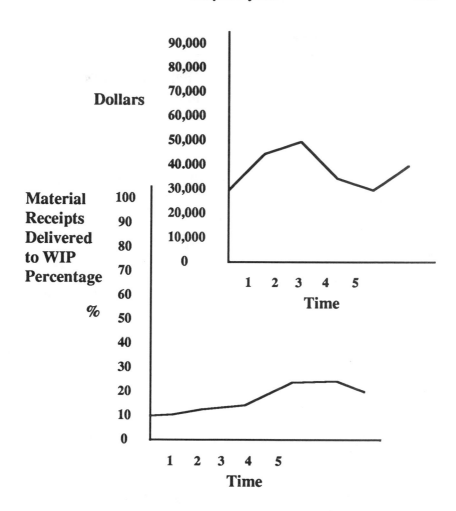

Price = Material dollars cost.

Carrying cost % = Computed carrying cost % of inventory per day.

Days = Days to get to the floor.

Number of Suppliers Certified

Purpose: Measurement should reflect the company's activity toward certification of their suppliers. In the beginning stages, the measurement could reflect the number of suppliers involved in the certification process.

Responsibility: All functions involved with the process of Supplier Certification should be concerned with this measurement. Management, Purchasing, Manufacturing, Quality, Engineering and Finance should have responsibility for accelerating this measurement.

Reporting: This measurement should be depicted in a graph maintained and displayed by the certification team.

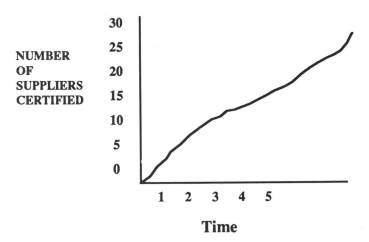

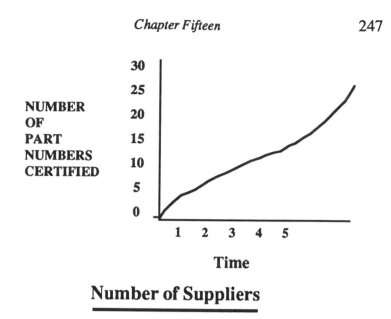

Time

Number of Suppliers

Purpose: This measurement should show the number of suppliers currently being utilized. Each represents a cost to source, prepare P.O., certify, process invoices and pay. The goal is to reduce the number of suppliers and thus reduce cost.

Responsibility: Purchasing should be responsible for this measurement.But, all functions of the company, including manufacturing, engineering, administration and management, should participate in the reduction. Management's responsibility should be on cost and on education about how to reduce.

Reporting: The measurement should be reflected in graphs and reports. Graphs should emphasize numbers and dollars. Reports should reflect dollars by function raher than as a part of the purchasing budget.

Calculation of Dollars:
Dollars = Processing cost x # of suppliers.
$45,000 = $120 x 375.

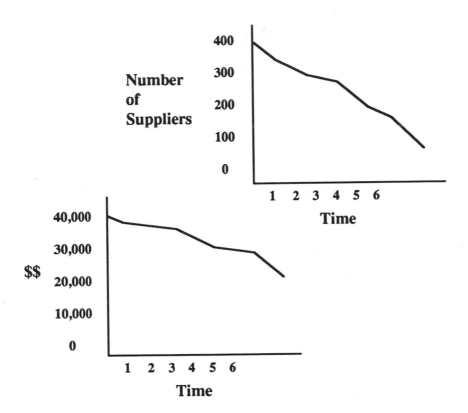

Processing cost = Time x material.

$120 = $40 x $3.

Processing time (labor) = Sourcing + P.O. + receiver + updating
inventory + invoice + voucher + check + reconciliation
+ changes (on all of the above).

$40 = $8/hr x 5 hrs.

Materials = All internal and external documents used to conduct
business with suppliers.

Note: Measurement is not to the bottom line. Instead, it empha-
sizes the need to reduce suppliers.

MANUFACTURING MEASUREMENTS

Material Moves

Purpose: The movement of materials through the company is non-productive and therefore waste. Movement in and out of inventory, from one operation to another and from plant to warehouse needs to be identified, analyzed and then eliminated.

Responsibility: Each function that deals with materials should be asking itself how the material arrives and where the next receiving area is. These functions need to take responsibility for finding ways to reduce the effort and the time it takes to move material through the company. This measurement should include non-material moves such as engineering change orders, invoices, production schedules and packing slips.

Reporting: Measurements should be represented on a graph showing the time involved in moving something.

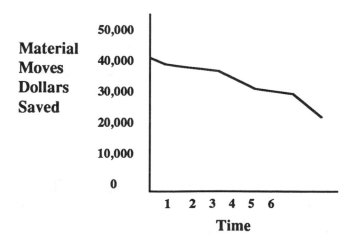

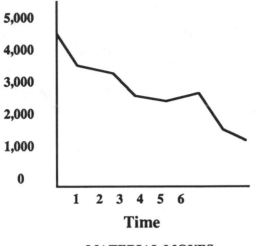

MATERIAL MOVES
NUMBER OF MOVES

Calculation of Dollars:

Material moves into and out of inventory = Parts x average
moves. (Computer transactions should provide number
of moves and number of parts.)
9,000 = 3,000 parts x 3 average moves.

Dollars to move = $5. (Represents estimate of labor and equip-
ment usage.)

Total dollars = Parts x average moves x dollars to move.
$45,000 = 3,000 x 3 x $5.

Note: Dollars are not to the bottom line, but are reflected in
overhead and should be used to emphasize the need to reduce the
number of moves in a **World Class** operation.

Scrap and Rework

Purpose: Both scrap and rework represent waste to **World Class** efforts. They indicate a company's inability to produce a product right the first time. Measurements allow the company to note improvement in reducing this waste.

Responsibility: To determine responsibility, the company must first determine why scrap and rework is produced. The causes need to be identified, displayed with the use of a Pareto chart and the root causes eliminated by the responsible function.

Reporting: Measurements need to be recorded in both reports and graphs. Graphs make visible the severity of the problem and the amount of dollars lost. Reports reflect the opportunity to reduce cost through the elimination of waste.

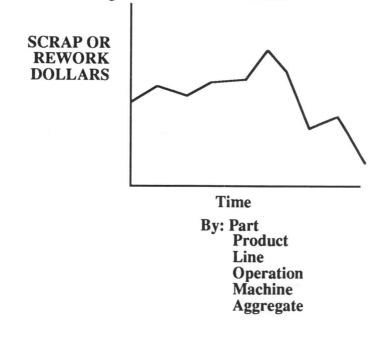

**SCRAP OR
REWORK
DOLLARS**

Time

**By: Part
Product
Line
Operation
Machine
Aggregate**

Set-Up Reduction

Purpose: Set-up reduction measurements show a company's improvement in several ways. We first want to perform set-up in less time. Then, as we reduce the time, we should also reduce the lot size. By reducing lot size, the company can be more flexible in the production mix needed to meet real customer requirements.

Responsibility: Set-up reduction needs to be attacked through the use of teams. Teams are responsible for achieving continuous goals of a 50 percent reduction on a no cost/ low cost effort.

Reporting: Measurements for set-up reduction should be reported in graphs and reports. Graphs reflect minutes and hours reduced, lot size reduction, productivity improvements, inventory reduction and cost savings. Reports should reflect cost reduction and increased unit production.

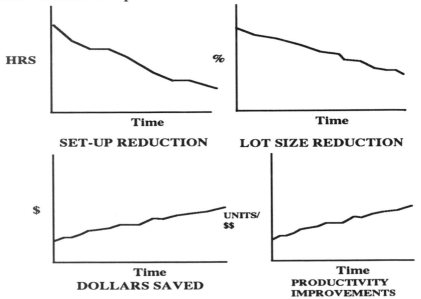

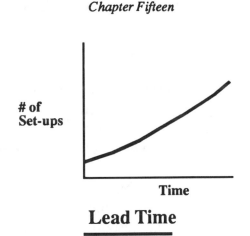

of
Set-ups

Time

Lead Time

Purpose: This measurement allows the facility to track conformance to stated lead times. It should reflect the effort made in reducing lead time, an important goal of **World Class** manufacturers.

Responsibility: The operations function should be responsible for capturing the necessary data. All elements of lead time should be included, such as : Order entry, Job entry, Purchasing, Kitting, Queue, Set-up, Run (machine and/or labor), Wait, Move, Shipping functions (including paperwork) and In-transit times.

Reporting: Reports should indicate product performance reductions. A benchmark should be established and goals set to be measured against.

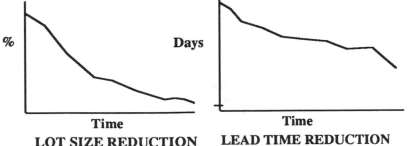

%   Days

Time   Time
LOT SIZE REDUCTION   **LEAD TIME REDUCTION**

Uptime

Purpose: Uptime represents any unplanned stoppage of manufacturing operations. The stoppage could be an issue with a machine, material, documentation or people. Regardless of the reason, downtime is a waste and must be recognized, monitored and eliminated.

Responsibility: The operations function must react as quickly as possible to direct the necessary resources for resolving the issue.

Reporting: To obtain the data for this measurement, it is necessary for someone to log the time from work stoppage until the operation is up and running at normal operating efficiency. Reports and graphs should reflect hours and dollars lost. Dollars should show both labor and lost production.

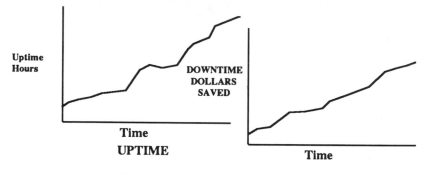

SALES MEASUREMENTS

On-Time Delivery to Customers

Purpose: This measurement is in place to insure performance to the customer's stated lead time. It should reflect variances to the delivery date whether the delivery is an hour late or early.

Responsibility: Sales should be responsible for insuring that delivery dates are possible within the facility's ability to schedule, manufacture and ship. Sales should monitor results of this measurement and facilitate the corrections of all variances and notify customers of performance.

Reporting: This measurement should be updated to reflect daily, weekly or monthly results. Reports should contain percentages, average days and cost of non-conformance. Special handling and premium freight should be included in the cost.

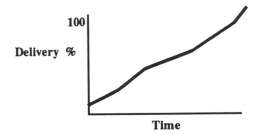

Customer Complaints

Purpose: The purpose of this measurement is to insure that the facility is reacting to customer complaints. All complaints should be logged in categories such as the following: Delivery, Quality, Quantity, Packaging, Billing and Service.

Responsibility: It is the responsibility of Sales to insure that all complaints are identified, investigated and get resolved by the appropriate functions on a timely basis.

Reporting: This measurement should reflect the number of complaints and a Pareto chart by category. The cost of non-conformance should also be included as the inquiry cost to track each complaint.

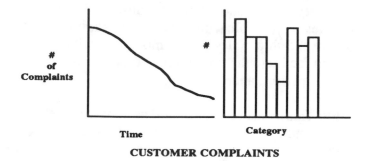

CUSTOMER COMPLAINTS

MANAGEMENT MEASUREMENTS

Cost vs. Benefits

Purpose: This measurement allows management to track the progress of continuous improvement programs. All costs expended for programs are measured against cost savings realized.

Responsibility: Responsibility lies with the teams or project leaders to capture the data from their programs and to summarize totals for management. Some goal or period of time should be established for the point at which benefits outweigh costs.

Reporting: This measurement should be in the form of a graph which is manually prepared from data captured by the teams.

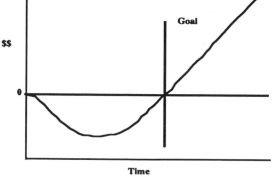

COST VS. PROFIT

Calculation of Dollars:
Cost (Spending) = Labor + material + overhead.
Benefit (Savings) = Labor + material + overhead.
Total = Benefit - cost.

Inventory Turnover

Purpose: This measurement allows management to track how efficiently the company is using their inventory investment. The goal is to increase the number of inventory turns continuously.

Responsibility: It should be management's responsiblity to direct the company's efforts at reducing inventory to levels where material is acutally being used, rather than just sitting.

Reporting: In order to present management with the best opportunity to reduce inventory, turnover rates should be reported at the product level for all inventory. Include obsolete and slow-moving inventory in this measurement as well, since it is also being managed. Raw material, WIP and Finished Goods must be included to truly track company turn ratios.

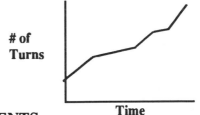

of
Turns

Time

QUALITY MEASUREMENTS

Incoming Parts Inspected

Purpose: This measurement reflects the ability of a company to work with its suppliers to receive defect-free parts and toward completely eliminating incoming inspection.

Responsibility: Responsibility should be with the Supplier Certification team and Quality function. Every effort should be made to obtain zero-defect parts and eliminate inspection techniques.

Reporting: This measurement should take the form of a graph which represents the percentage of parts still being inspected. Reports can reflect the dollars expended on inspection for individual products and as an aggregate number.

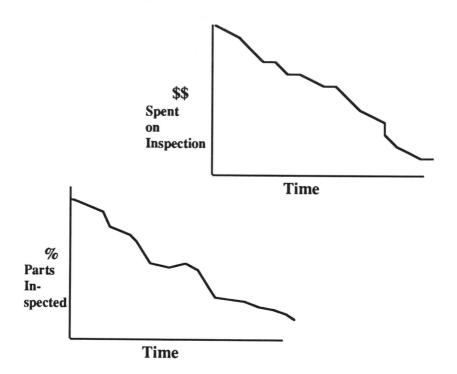

Calculation of dollars:

Dollars spent = Labor + material + equipment.

Other Quality Measurements

- **Number of Floor Parts Inspected.**

- **Hours of Inspection.**

- **Operations under SPC.**

- **Operators Trained in SPC.**

- **Training Hours and Dollars per Employee.**

- **Cost of Quality.**

- **Material Acquisition Cost.**

ADMINISTRATIVE MEASUREMENT

Voucher Error

Purpose: A **World Class** company looks to all departments for improvement. Measuring voucher errors illustrates visibility into Accounts Payable and identifies areas of improvement.

Responsibility: The responsibility for this measurement should be with the individuals performing the voucher entry function. Accountability for vouchering should be with the Accounts Payable department team.

Reporting: Changes made to vouchers can be collected manually or through a computer system which already logs them.

There are numerous measurements mentioned in this book, both in this chapter and throughout the functional area. Measuring a company's success and present position provides both a "shap-shot" in time and a vehicle for improvement. We are sure that there are many other measurements which exist in each company today. Our concern is that they conflict with reaching **World Class** status. Discarding traditional methods of measuring is painful. Each company will spend hours arguing what should and shouldn't stay. The challenge is to measure numerous tasks in the beginning and, as progress is achieved, to measure only the areas which continually require improvement.

We did not try to include every possible index, formula or ratio that exists. We did include those key measurements, which if not measured, will result in failure on your journey to World Class. The Performance Measurement Chart on the following page-should serve as a guide in establishing the overall measurement process.

PERFORMANCE MEASUREMENT CHART

	JAN	FEB	MAR	APR		OCT	NOV	DEC	AVG %	LEV-EL	Goal
Business											
Operation											
Administra-tion											
Accuracy											
Management											
Marketing & Sales											
Value Ana-lyst											

CHAPTER SIXTEEN

The Malcolm Baldrige National Quality Award

The purpose of the Malcolm Baldrige National Quality Award, in the words of a 1988 winner, is to help "American companies become world class." We couldn't agree more with this statement which was made by John C. Marous, Chairman and Chief Executive Officer of Westinghouse Electric Corp., whose subsidiary, Westinghouse Commercial Nuclear Fuels Division, won the award in the manufacturing category.

The award, which contains a medal bearing the legend "The Quest for Excellence," is the United States' equivalent of Japan's Deming Prize for Quality. The Baldrige Award is the highest accolade for quality that an American company can receive. It was created by Congress in 1987 and named in honor of Secretary of

Commerce Malcolm Baldrige who died that year in a rodeo accident. The award was, however, actually conceived by Florida Power and Light Company, a Miami-based private company which pushed for the establishment of the award. Currently, the award is administered and funded by a group of private companies and is managed by the Commerce Department's National Institute of Standards and Technology.

In its third year, the number of applicants climbed to 97, double the amount in 1989. Among the applicants are NeXT, Inc., Texas Instruments and Westinghouse. Past winners have reported that their sales people are welcomed much more quickly now that the company has won the award. It is obvious that the Baldrige Award has grown considerably in importance.

WHY THE AWARD WAS ESTABLISHED

According to the May 22, 1989 issues of *Business America*, a publication of the Commerce Department, the award was established to:

- "Formally recognize companies for quality leadership and permit them to advertise receipt of their awards.

- Encourage companies to improve their quality management practices in order to compete for future awards.

- Develop award criteria that U.S. companies can refer to for quality improvement guideline.

- Share quality strategies of the award recipients with the U.S. industry."

As you can see, the Baldrige Award was designed to increase the **World Class** awareness of the whole country and to publicize companies that have achieved **World Class Status.** It is hoped that their efforts will be emulated by other companies in the United States.

QUALIFYING FOR THE AWARD

To win the Baldrige Award, a company must complete up to 75 pages of criteria and answer over 133 questions about quality. Those who pass this tier are then subject to a three-day, on-site examination. The criteria are very rigorous and emphasize both quality achievements and systems for quality improvement.

Your company is eligible to vie for this award if it is incorporated and located in the United States. The company can be either public or private. The Baldrige Award is given in three categories: 1) Large manufacturing companies or subsidiaries, 2) Large service companies and 3) Smaller companies (independently owned and under 500 full-time employees) either in manufacturing or service. The rules allow for up to two winners in each category.

Whatever the category, award examiners consider seven criteria. The list below and point totals are from the award booklet:

100 Maximum Points
- Leadership — The senior management's success in creating and sustaining a quality culture.

60 Maximum Points
- Information and analysis — The effectiveness of the company's collection and analysis of information for quality improvement and planning.

90 Maximum Points
- Planning — The effectiveness of integration of quality requirements into the company's business plans.

150 Maximum Points
- Human Resource Utilization — The success of the company's efforts to utilize the full potential of the work force for quality.

150 Maximum Points
- Quality Assurance — The effectiveness of the company's systems for assuring quality control of all operations.

150 Maximum Points
- Quality Assurance Results — The company's results in quality achievements and quality improvement, demonstrated through quantitative measures.

300 Maximum Points
- Customer Satisfaction — The effectiveness of the company's systems to determine customer requirements and demonstrated success in meeting them. Finalists are subject to an on-site visit by examiners to verify their quality programs.

Total Maximum Points = 1,000

THE APPLICATION PROCESS

After the application is submitted by a company, the 130-member Board of Examiners selects at least four members to review and evaluate an application. Companies which score high are then eligible for on-site visits by one or more teams of examiners which are comprised of experts in quality from universities, industry and professional/trade associations.

As we stated, the on-site visit lasts two or three days. Its purpose is to verify the application's contents. While visiting a company's departments, records are reviewed and corporate officials are interviewed with the idea of getting up-to-date information about the company. Most important, however, is the examiners assessment of the adoption of company culture focused on quality implementation.

The examining teams then prepare a report which they submit to a panel of nine judges. These judges are entrusted with the task of recommending award recipients to the National Institute of Standards and Technology and the Secretary of Commerce.

For further information about the Baldrige Award and the application process, write to:

Malcolm Baldrige National Quality Award
National Institute of Standards and Technology
Gaithersburg, MD 20899.
Tel: (301) 975-2036

HOW PAST WINNERS WON THE AWARD

Motorola Inc.

Motorola began its quest for **World Class** when it adopted **the** objective of "Total Customer Satisfaction." The company's goal was:

"Zero defects in everything we do."

One of the practices they implemented to achieve this goal was enforcing the requirement that all corporate officials and business managers wear pagers. This way, whenever a customer called with a complaint, the managers were available. Managers were also required to visit their customers regularly in order to get first-hand knowledge of what they liked and disliked about Motorola products and service. To this end, the company also gathered information through customer hotlines, surveys and field audits.

As for quality, Motorola started with the goal of getting a tenfold reduction in defects within five years. Within two years, they were so close to achieving the goal that the company decided to push for a hundredfold reduction in errors. That goal was reached sooner than expected as well. Now, Motorola has instituted the Six Sigma program. Six Sigma is a statistical term. It states that there will be no more than 3.4 defects per million no matter what the process of procedure.

It should be noted that Motorola has implemented their quality programs in all areas of the company, not only the production floor. That means office functions, customer service and product design and many, many more areas.

Motorola spends up to $100 million a year on employee training. About forty percent is devoted to procedures and skills needed to build a perfect product or provide error-free service. Motorola has now seized the No. 1 spot in the cut-throat Japanese pager market. They have now directed their supply base to apply for the Baldrige Award. Applying for the award stands for your effort in quality and shows you are doing what it takes to become **World Class.**

We, at Pro-Tech, are extremely proud to be part of the faculty at Motorola University. Motorola's training and educational institute was founded to further the education of employees throughout the company.

Commercial Nuclear Fuel Division
Westinghouse Electric Corporation

Westinghouse's Commercial Nuclear Fuels Division (CNFD) determined early in their quality program that they would need to make the best fuel rods in the world in order to win a bigger share of the world market. Like many companies, they had been happy when only 95 percent of their products were perfect. They now accept only 99.995 percent quality and are striving to do better.

CNFD has succeeded because they began using statistical techniques to track progress and monitor control in 60 crucial areas which they call "Pulse Points." Combined with state-of-the-art technology such as robotics and laser welding, they have achieved 100 percent on-time delivery of high-quality products.

CNFD also maintains almost daily contact with its customers. Data is gathered at utilities to evaluate the performance of its fuel assemblies in the field.

Globe Metallurgical Inc.

Globe's goal was **World Class** right from the start — to be the lowest cost, highest quality producer in the world. Globe, like other winners, used statistical process control in their quality efforts. They made the further requirement that each person in the company was responsible for charting their own data. The rationale was that people would get a better feel for what needed to be done. The company was absolutely right.

Productivity was up 30 percent. Customer complaints dropped by 91 percent. Globe reports that in 1987 none of its ferroalloy and silicon metal was returned for replacement. In addition, their accident rate has fallen below the average for the industry in 1985, while the industry average rose. And, as an example of employee commitment, absenteeism has also decreased.

Xerox Corporation Business Products and Systems and Milliken & Company

Training and education were the keys to Xerox and Milliken winning the 1989 awards in the manufacturing category. Xerox put more than 4 million hours and $125 million into a project to present quality principles to its employees. Milliken spent over $1,300 per employee in its training and education program. The quality teams, which are self-managed, have enabled Milliken to eliminate nearly 700 management positions.

Florida Power and Light

Proving that service companies can excel at quality control, Florida Power and Light (FPL) became the first company outside of Japan to win the coveted Deming Prize. Like Milliken and Xerox, FPL devoted many hours and financial resources to its program. Volunteer quality teams learned a number of statistical methods such as Pareto charts and histograms in their efforts to become **World Class.**

WHY QUALITY IS VITAL TO WORLD CLASS STATUS

I think you can agree that there are some common denominators in the actions of the winners above. All stated that achieving **World Class** requires:

- **Strong leadership.**

- **Well-defined goals.**

- **Company-wide commitment.**

- **Training and education.**

As I have repeatedly stated as well, quality sells. The achievement of **World Class** does mean reduced costs, top quality and increased market share.

CHAPTER SEVENTEEN

Why the Achievement
of World Class Status
Is Important

On your journey toward achieving **World Class Status**, bear in mind that early successes can be misleading. Early success must not be accepted as completion of the process. There is no greater disappointment in the world of business than being witness to a company that implements a program and then fails to capitalize on its results by expanding the process. It's like qualifying for the Olympics and then deciding not to compete. Improvement is a continuous process which supports **World Class Status** and, once there, explores more efficient and flexible methods for satisfying a customer's specifications and growing demands, 100 percent of the time.

Achieving World Class Status or the Baldrige Award provides a future for our people. I seriously question the success or survival probability of any company which does not involve people at all levels. Companies which have the mentality of not granting responsibility and authority to their people are headed for extinction. Remember the old saying:

Innovate, Emigrate or Evaporate.

World Class Status is about survival. Competition drives the process. Annual reports often contain the statement that "people are our most valuable asset." **World Class** companies employ this statement through teams which are empowered to make changes necessary for continuous improvement.

CONTINUOUS IMPROVEMENT PROCESS

Progress toward the goal of **World Class Status** begins with a mind-set of not meeting the competition, but of

"Being the Best."

Top management commitment means building an environment where creative problem-solving is the norm. Furthermore, it means squarely confronting the most difficult task of management—team work and people involvement. This can be accomplished when management establishes goals and objectives and exercises patience and persistence. It will require the development of trust with your people, suppliers and customers and the delegation of responsibility and authority to the lowest levels of the organization.

Why don't you take the challenge yourself? Commit your company to winning.

There is no question in the minds of the staff of Professionals for Technology that we can achieve **World Class Status**. The complex problems which face us in the future cry out for more improvements. They will require a company's commitment, dedication, drive and ambition to be the best.

There is
no end!

BIBLIOGRAPHY

MADE IN AMERICA: *The Total Business Concept*,
(ISBN 0-945456-00-X) by Peter L. Grieco, Jr. and Michael W.
Gozzo, PT Publications, Inc., Suite 105, 4360 North Lake
Blvd., Palm Beach Gardens, FL 33410.

JUST-IN-TIME PURCHASING: *In Pursuit of Excellence*,
(ISBN 0-945456-01-8) by Peter L. Grieco, Jr., Michael W.
Gozzo and Jerry W. Claunch, PT Publications, Inc., Suite 105,
4360 North Lake Blvd., Palm Beach Gardens, FL 33410.

SUPPLIER CERTIFICATION: *Achieving Excellence*,
(ISBN 0-945456-02-6) by Peter L. Grieco, Jr., Michael W.
Gozzo and Jerry W. Claunch, PT Publications, Inc., Suite 105,
4360 North Lake Blvd., Palm Beach Gardens, FL 33410.

BEHIND BARS: *Bar Coding Principles and Applications*,
(ISBN 0-945456-03-4) by Peter L. Grieco, Jr., Michael W.
Gozzo and C.J. (Chip) Long, PT Publications, Inc., Suite 105,
4360 North Lake Blvd., Palm Beach Gardens, FL 33410.

SET-UP REDUCTION: *Saving Dollars with Common Sense*,
(ISBN 0-945456-04-2) by Jerry W. Claunch and Philip D.
Stang, PT Publications, Inc., Suite 105, 4360 North Lake Blvd.,
Palm Beach Gardens, FL 33410.

JIT/TQC LEARNING INSTRUMENT, M. Scott Myers,
Center for Applied Management.

ANSWERS TO JIT//TQC QUIZ

#1 — "g"
#2 — all, except for "p" and "u"
#3 — "e"
#4 — all
#5 — all
#6 — all
#7 — "j"
#8 — all
#9 — "e"
#10 — all
#11 — all
#12 — all
#13 — "a"
#14 — "b" - "e"
#15 — "d"
#16 — Sitting = "a" - "c", "f" - "h", "k";
        Moving = "d", "e", "i", "j", "l"
#17 — "a"
#18 — all
#19 — "a", "b", "d", "e"
#20 — "a"
#21 — "a" - "e"
#22 — "a" = Logistical, "b" = Behavioral,
        "c" = Environmental, "d" = Leadership
#23 — "e"
#24 — "a"

#25 — "b"
#26 — "e"
#27 — "e"
#28 — "a"
#29 — "b", "d"
#30 — "a" - "g", "i"
#31 — "b" - "g"
#32 — "a", "c", "e", "k", "m", "q" - "s"
#33 — "b", "c"
#34 — all
#35 — all except "h"
#36 — "a"
#37 — "c"
#38 — "a"
#39 — "b"
#40 — "a"
#41 — 5, 1, 6, 4, 3, 2
#42 — "a", "c" - "e", "h"
#43 — all
#44 — "a"
#45 — "b" = 3, "d" = 4, "e" = 1, "g" = 2, "h" = 5
#46 — triangle, arrow, half circle, square, circle
#47 — "h"
#48 — Add Value = "c", "e", "h"
          Add Cost = "a', "b", "d", "f", "g", "i"
#49 — all
#50 — all
#51 — "e"
#52 — "c"
#53 — all, except "c"
#54 — all

INDEX